MEMORY ENHANC
IN 30 DAYS

By the same authors:

HAVE AN OUT-OF-BODY EXPERIENCE IN 30 DAYS
HIGHER CONSCIOUSNESS IN 30 DAYS
INNER SEX IN 30 DAYS
LUCID DREAMS IN 30 DAYS
RIGHT-BRAIN LEARNING IN 30 DAYS

MEMORY ENHANCEMENT IN 30 DAYS

THE TOTAL-RECALL PROGRAMME

**KEITH HARARY &
PAMELA WEINTRAUB**

Aquarian/Thorsons
An Imprint of HarperCollins*Publishers*

The Aquarian Press
An Imprint of HarperCollins*Publishers*
77–85 Fulham Palace Road,
Hammersmith, London W6 8JB

First published by St Martin's Press, New York, 1991
This edition published by The Aquarian Press 1992

10 9 8 7 6 5 4 3 2 1

A catalogue record for this book
is available from the British Library

ISBN 1 85538 240 7

Printed in Great Britain by
Mackays of Chatham, Kent

For Jerry and Katharine Posner, who remember that we're all the same age in the middle of the night.
—Keith Harary

For the Crack, Indian Quad, and Kenmore Square—not the places, but the memories of the states of mind.
—Pamela Weintraub

CONTENTS

INTRODUCTION

Memory plays a vital role in your life. In fact, your ability to remember your own life experience not only determines your notion of reality, but also your sense of who you are.

Just take a few minutes to reflect on what your life would be like if you were somehow struck with amnesia—how could you know how to act without a clear notion of where you had come from or what had happened the year or the week before? On the other hand, suppose that your memory was flawless—so flawless and unfading, in fact, that you found it impossible to forget even the tiniest details of your daily existence. Finally, suppose that you had only an extremely short-term memory and had to be introduced to your family, friends, and co-workers over and over again every five minutes.

For most of us, of course, these rare memory problems are purely theoretical. Yet they do provide some insight into the power that memory—or lack of it—has over our lives. To be sure, memory is much more than merely tying a string around your finger to remember an appointment. As psychologists point out, your long-term memories—perhaps dating back to your birth—can affect the most minor as well as the most significant dimensions of your relationships with others. Your short-term memories can also have a profound effect on the quality of your everyday life. Anyone who has ever had the embarrassing experience of bumping into a recent business contact on the street and not being able to place his or her face knows how profound problems with short-term memory can be.

In *Memory Enhancement in 30 Days: The Total-Recall Program*, you will learn how to hone your memory—telescoping it to absorb the broad strokes of your life, and reigning it in to record the tiniest details with precision and ease. The driving principle behind our memory technique is the conviction that memory is an inner, associative process. Although we often tend to think of memory merely as a matter of recording logical facts and figures in our mental files for later retrieval, memory is not necessarily experienced in a linear fashion at all. For instance, you no doubt often find yourself responding to current situations by falling into *memory patterns* of the past. The more outwardly logical aspects of situations can all but disappear as these misplaced memory patterns take hold.

Memory is also a multisensory phenomenon. Memories of various smells and tastes, for instance, can affect everything from your response to a smoldering fire in the walls of your apartment to your emotional response to a home-cooked meal.

In the thirty days of the Total-Recall Program, you will, first of all, develop a greater personal awareness of how memory affects your life. You will also use this awareness to enhance your memory for performance in sports events, recollection of lecture material, and social ease.

You will start, in Week One, by exploring your memory of the past. In this section, entitled "The Remembered Self," you will tap into your impressions of your birth, childhood, and adolescence.

In Week Two, "The Doors of Perception," you will hone your sensual memory one sensory modality at a time. Focusing on a variety of fabricated experiences, you will learn how to sharpen your memory of visual, auditory, tactile, and olfactory cues.

In Week Three, "Right-Brain Memory," you will focus on enhancing your memory through the associative, creative, intuitive aspect of your brain. By tapping these nonanalytic tools, which some researchers have associated with the right brain, you should be able to remember faces and events with the aid of your unconscious mind. You will, for instance, learn how to tune into the memory clues in your dreams and focus all your senses on an event as it unfolds. Tapping relaxation and visualization techniques, you will also learn how to etch the memory of an important event into your mind.

Finally, in Week Four, "Total Recall," you will learn how to track and preserve memories so that you can hold on to them for the rest of your life.

As you work your way through *Memory Enhancement in 30 Days: The Total-Recall Program,* please proceed at your own pace. You do not have to complete this book in exactly thirty days. You can take as long as you like to complete the program, adapting it to fit your particular personal needs. We do not, however, recommend completing the program in fewer than thirty days, since we doubt you would experience the full benefit of each exercise at that pace.

You are about to begin the Total-Recall Program. We hope you will enjoy the memorable experiences to come.

WEEK ONE

THE REMEMBERED SELF

WEEK ONE

•

THE REMEMBERED SELF

*H*ave you ever stopped to consider the difference between who you were as a child and the individual you have since become? In the years that have passed since you were five years old, your understanding of the everyday world has certainly gone through some major transformations. Back then, five years was literally your entire life. By the time you'd reached age ten, a mere five years later, you had already doubled the period of your own worldly existence and experienced critical changes in your perspective on reality.

From the vantage point of adulthood, however, five years may seem far less substantial. Instead of measuring the passing time through shifts in your sense of self, you might measure it merely by the pounds you have gained or the extra money you earn. Looking back on the period of your earliest childhood, you may find it difficult to consciously connect who you are now with who you were then, yet your memories of your earliest life undoubtedly affect you today.

During Week One of the Total-Recall Program you will strive to recall your earliest self. You will attempt to reconstruct impressions of birth, to recall the feelings and emotions of childhood, and to commune with the childhood qualities that you've managed to sustain. You will, in short, be getting in touch with your own forgotten self.

As you recall your forgotten self, you should come to better understand who and what you are. You should also generate memory touchstones to help you comprehend—and thus, better recall—the events of your present, day-to-day life.

DAY 1

WOMB WITH A VIEW

Are reported birth memories pure fantasy, as some researchers have suggested, or is the recollection of life's earliest experience really possible? Although you may find it difficult to believe that bona fide memories can register in the newly born, many psychologists and medical professionals claim to have convincing evidence of the phenomenon. To assist you in exploring this possibility, the first two days of the Total-Recall Program offer some simple exercises for inducing the memory—or at least the subjective feelings and impressions—of your life as a fetus in the womb and your subsequent birth.

Our first birth exercise—"Womb With a View"—was suggested by obstetrician Rene Van de Carr, president of Prenatal University in Hayward, California. To begin, learn as much as you can about your mother's pregnancy, including the details of your delivery. Van de Carr reminds us that whatever medication your mother received before you were born was also received by you, so you should consider how this may have influenced your feelings—particularly during your passage from the womb.

Mental Note—Because the second phase of today's exercise requires some preparation, please read ahead through the rest of the instructions before you continue.

For the next phase of today's exercise, choose a quiet time when you can relax in a warm bathtub in the dark without being disturbed for at least thirty minutes. Before getting into the water, turn on a radio at low volume between stations so you hear soothing static but no voices or music. Then get into the tub, take a deep breath, and get comfortable. (Unless you have a radio made specifically for the shower or bath, be careful not to place the radio anywhere near the water; avoid fiddling with the dials once you get into the bath.)

The darkness, warm water, and radio static (also called "white noise") are intended to simulate the conditions you experienced before birth and allow you to imagine yourself returning to the moment your conscious awareness first began. As you sit in the bathtub in the dark, feeling the warmth of your aquatic surroundings soaking into your body, allow any thoughts or concerns about your present existence to drift from your mind. Focus only on your physical sensations and the sound of the static in the background.

Consider the experience of your own prenatal development and birth. Imagine that your body has suddenly become much smaller and that the darkness and water surrounding you comprise your entire world. Take your time and allow yourself to experience fully the secure familiarity of this womblike environment.

After you have focused on these initial feelings and sensations for a comfortable period of time, remember—or if, like most people, you can't remember, envision—emerging from darkness into bright lights. Imagine being surrounded by people incredibly enormous compared with yourself. Re-create, at least in your imagination, your own experience of being born. As you do so, you should eventually lift yourself out of the water, dry yourself off, and turn on a light. Then find a warm and comfortable place to wrap yourself up in a sheet or blanket for at least twenty minutes, and reflect upon and fully absorb the impact of this experience.

> **Mental Note**—Even if you don't find yourself getting in touch with the sensations of gestation and birth the first time you practice this exercise, at the very least, Van de Carr says, you should be able to enjoy a period of peace and quiet. If you practice this exercise just before going to sleep, you may find yourself having dreams that deal, in some fashion, with the birth experience.

DAY 2

FETAL ATTRACTION

Like the Day 1 exercise, the exercise suggested for Day 2 should help you get in touch with the general sensations of birth. Suggested by Toronto psychiatrist Thomas Verny, coauthor with Pamela Weintraub of *Nurturing the Unborn Child*, this exercise should carry yesterday's experience one step further by triggering still more elaborate birth-related images and sensations.

> **Mental Note**—Please read ahead through the rest of the instructions for Day 2 before you continue.

To conduct today's exercise, you'll need a book of photographs showing the developmental progress of the human fetus at twenty-eight days, two months, three months, four months, and so on. Lennart Nilsson's book, *A Child Is Born*, is highly recommended, although any similar text showing color photographs of embryonic development will suffice.

Begin by sitting alone in a quiet, comfortable place, where you can later lie down and listen to some baroque or other classical music. Take your time and relax, spending at least twenty to thirty minutes looking through the photographs in the book. As you do so, imagine that you are gazing at images of your own prenatal development, and notice the impact this may have on your emotions. Stay focused on your feelings as you continue flipping through the pictures and trying to reconstruct—in your imagination, if not your memory—your experience as a developing fetus.

> *Mental Note*—For an especially powerful variation of this technique, you may wish to conduct this exercise in a bathtub filled with warm water as you did on Day 1. Once again, take all appropriate precautions to avoid handling a radio, tape recorder, or any other electrical device while lying in the bath.

Lie down, get comfortable, and play a classical record or tape that is at least thirty minutes long. Any classical orchestral music will do, although Mozart, Vivaldi, or Schubert should be particularly effective. As you listen, focus on your memories of the photographs you studied earlier, and on any spontaneous thoughts and images they may have triggered. Don't pressure yourself into feeling anything in particular. Instead, just relax, allow your thoughts to flow with the music, and remember any feelings the photographs inspired. Then close your eyes and imagine that the music is carrying you back to the womb.

> *Mental Note*—This exercise may or may not trigger what some psychologists call a "major birth memory." Rather than a technicolor, cinematic scene, you might simply glimpse a color or image or recall a texture or sound associated with being born. At the very least, this exercise should help you visualize what it felt like to be in the womb. This guided imagery exercise, Verny says, can help you see that even though birth was difficult, you have overcome it. It can thus inspire you to overcome difficult situations as an adult.

Mental Note—If your experience with this exercise has been a positive one, you may wish to repeat it in about a week. Often the images generated by this exercise build on each other, so that a more complete picture of your prenatal experience may eventually start to emerge. For this reason, we'll remind you to practice this entire exercise again one week from today.

DAY 3

THE EYES OF A CHILD

There is, of course, much more to reviving your early life memories than focusing on gestation and birth. Some of your most significant life experiences, now residing in your deepest memories, more than likely occurred in your childhood. This is a basic premise underlying much of psychoanalysis, not to mention the entire field of psychology. But it is not necessary to go through years of psychotherapy—nor to recall unpleasant or traumatic events—in order to get back in touch with some meaningful childhood memories that may have had a powerful impact on your adult life. As far as we're concerned, in fact, all that's required is a change in perspective. Instead of looking at the world through the eyes of an adult, you may, for a time at least, view the world the way you once did, through the eyes of a child.

On Day 3, therefore, you will focus on communicating on a deep, internal level with remembered impressions of yourself in the distant past. By communicating directly with the child within—the part of yourself many contemporary psychologists now call "the inner child"—you may rediscover personal dreams and goals that have long seemed lost. You can also learn to consciously share with your childhood self the greater wisdom of the adult you have since become.

Mental Note—If you have a history of psychiatric problems or feel at all uncomfortable about remembering your early life, we urge you to consult a mental-health professional before trying this approach or, for that matter, any of the exercises in Week One of the Total-Recall Program. This exercise should not be viewed as a form of psychotherapy or as a substitute for seeking firsthand professional psychological guidance when appropriate. Focusing on your childhood perspective toward reality and your own life can often generate surprisingly powerful emotions. We therefore also recommend that you take this exercise slowly and allow yourself time to fully absorb its impact.

To begin today's exercise, choose a meaningful spot where you spent at least one particularly thoughtful occasion alone as a child. If possible, go there. If the spot is too far away to visit conveniently, choose a substitute site that reminds you of the original. Or, you may simply sit alone in a quiet and dimly lit environment and visit the place in your imagination. The place you select does not need to be one you visited on a daily basis. A church, an attic room, or possibly the home of a favorite relative would be a suitable location, as would a playground, museum, backyard, pool hall, or a spot on the beach overlooking the ocean. (One person we know spent much of her childhood reflecting in the bathroom—the only room in her family's small apartment in which she could have any privacy. She went back to that bathroom and did this exercise there.) If the location you select is a large building, choose a more or less secluded spot within it, where you can sit quietly without being interrupted.

Take a deep breath, relax, and recall how you felt when you first visited this place as a child. Instead of merely analyzing your childhood feelings from the viewpoint of an adult, however, allow yourself to relive in your mind's eye your childhood experience as much as possible. To whatever extent you can, focus on the questions that were most important to you then.

Now imagine that time as we normally think of it does not exist, and that you can communicate directly with your childhood self. Exchange viewpoints with each other: As the child, tell the adult about things he or she may have forgotten, revealing your deepest desires and goals. As the adult, share with the child what you now know about life. Ask the child you once were to recall some worthwhile aspects of your personality or inner experience with which your adult self has lost touch.

Mental Note—As you practice this exercise, you may experience a sense of timelessness. You may, for instance, feel the apparent separation between past and present fade—as though your child and adult selves were both alive inside of you at once—which, in a psychological sense, they most likely are. The child's remembered insights may help soften some of the hardened or jaded parts of your adult personality. The adult point of view may help resolve some conflicted childhood feelings still residing within.

Mental Note—You may wish to enhance this exercise by playing music that you originally heard as a child. Allow the music to remind you of your childhood and use it to emotionally connect you with your own remembered past.

DAY 4
PHOTO REPLAY

On Day 4, you'll use old photographs to help you recapture hidden memories of your early life. To carry out today's exercise most effectively, you'll need to gather together as many photographs as you can from your childhood and young adult life.

Mental Note—If you find it impossible to gather the old photographs you should ideally use, you may still conduct this exercise by visualizing specific scenes from your early life as though they were photographic slides being projected on your imagination. Simply substitute these imagined scenes for actual photographs while following the instructions below.

Begin today's exercise by finding a private and comfortable spot at home where you can relax without being disturbed while looking at your face in a mirror. Place the photographs you've gathered to use in this exercise in a pile before you. Then take a deep breath and, as you let it out, allow yourself to let go of any superficial tension you may be feeling in your body. Gaze at the reflection of your face in the mirror and, as you do so, let your thoughts drift over the present-day circumstances of your life.

Rather than focusing your attention on highly specific or factual details of your present situation, focus instead on your more generalized emotions. Consider any ways in which your feelings toward your present life circumstances may seem at all familiar. We are not referring here to the fact that these emotions are bound to seem familiar because you experience them daily in your present life. We are referring, instead, to the ways in which your current emotional circumstances may hail back to the emotional ambience of your childhood or teenage years.

If you find yourself currently feeling a sense of compassion toward the less fortunate, for example, you may wish to consider the ways in which this feeling reminds you of similar feelings you may have had in the past. Perhaps you felt compassion toward some of the less popular children in your class or neighborhood, for example, or perhaps you felt like an "underdog" as a child, and vowed never to allow others to be treated as poorly as people treated you. If you find yourself feeling preoccupied with attaining financial security and collecting material things, on the other hand, you may connect this feeling with a sense of financial insecurity during your youth.

As you look at your face in the mirror and consider the present circumstances of your life, don't dwell in convoluted analytic detail on whatever feelings you experience. Simply review them, as if from a distance, relating them in a general sense to your early life.

For the next phase of today's exercise, turn your attention toward the photographs you've gathered. It is not necessary to review these photographs in any particular order. In fact, we recommend that you review them randomly to increase your likelihood of generating spontaneous and less predictable memories of your childhood and young adult life.

As you review the photographs, which will probably show scenes of your development at various stages, occasionally glance at your reflection in the mirror. Consider the fact that the person you see in the mirror is the same individual as the child in the photographs. Pay special attention to any feelings of nostalgia generated by reviewing the photographs. And note, especially, specific memories triggered by—but not directly depicted in—the photos at hand.

Take your time and allow these memories to become as vivid as possible, noticing the emotions triggered in response to these memories and relating these feelings—if it is comfortable and easy for you to do so—to any sense you may have of yourself in your present-day life. Spend at least thirty to sixty minutes reviewing the photographs and carrying out this phase of the session.

Complete today's exercise by putting the photographs away and making a conscious effort to let go of your feelings about the past, at least for the time being. Then go for a walk or enjoy some similar, easygoing activity to balance the emotional intensity of your photo replay.

DAY 5

THOSE WERE THE
DAYS

On Day 5, you'll balance the more internally focused exercises of the past four days with an interpersonal approach to reviving early memories. To carry out this exercise, you'll need to get in touch with a friend with whom you've had a relationship since you were a child or young adult. If such a friend is unavailable, simply choose someone who is available and who has known you for as long as possible. You should get together with your old friend in person, if you can do so, though this is not absolutely essential.

To conduct the exercise, you should ideally get together in or near the place where you and your friend first met. You might, for example, take a walk through your old neighborhood and visit your elementary school playground; you might even sit on the swings. You might go back to the roller-skating rink where you first bumped into each other or visit the summer cottage community where the two of you first learned to swim in a lake.

We understand, however, that arranging such a symbolic rendezvous may not always be possible—especially for friends who live in distant geographical locales. In this case, you and your friend can conduct this exercise in an extended telephone conversation or arrange to meet in some other location convenient to you both.

Let us be clear, however, that the focus of today's exercise is not merely to get together with your friend and passively reminisce about days gone by. It is, rather, to communicate with someone who really knows what kind of person you were as a child or young adult.

Begin by telling your friend that you would like his or her help in reminding you of the kind of person you seemed to be back when the two of you first met. Needless to say, this will probably become a two-way discussion in which you both explore your earliest impressions of each other.

You might begin your discussion by describing what was going on in each of your lives on the day you first met. (If you don't remember the precise day, think back to the general period and start your discussion from there.) You might bring up a mutual past experience that you never felt comfortable discussing after it occurred. You might also take this opportunity to discuss details that you couldn't reveal to each other at the time, but which you would like to talk about now. Perhaps you always secretly envied the color of your friend's hair, for example, or the way in which he or she seemed much more comfortable than you with the opposite sex. Perhaps you harbored a deep romantic crush on your friend. Or perhaps you were secretly the victim of abusive or mentally unstable parents and managed to keep this a secret from your friend throughout your childhood. If you can, reveal these secrets to your friend now.

> **Mental Note**—You should discuss such secrets only if you feel completely comfortable doing so. Do not pressure each other to reveal any aspects of your lives that you still do not wish to discuss.

You might also ask your friend to describe his or her impression of you during that early time. What type of person were you? Did you seem to be happy or often depressed? Were you outgoing, or did you prefer to keep to yourself and a few close friends? Were you ruminative and philosophical, or did you love parties and having fun? Were you timid or adventurous? Were you interested in art and music, calculus and chemistry, or games and sports? Did your friend expect you to end up mired in anonymity in the suburbs, or did you seem destined for splashy greatness and success?

As you talk, encourage your old friend to probe deeply. Have him or her remind you of specific moments when your true personality—your real "inner self"—came through. Was there something your friend always wanted to tell you, but never felt safe about suggesting? Are there certain moments in your mutual past that either you or your friend treasure as especially valued memories? In what ways do your friend's memories and perceptions of those past experiences differ from your own?

After you and your friend have covered the material above, we'd like you to dwell on the changes you've both experienced since you last met. Are there aspects of your personality that your friend believes have been transformed, submerged, or even obliterated through the years? Has your recent meeting revealed new aspects of your personality, of which your friend was unaware? Are there aspects of your personality that remain eternal, no matter what you've been through or how much you've apparently changed?

If your friend describes aspects of your personality that strike you as somehow "off the mark," consider that every relationship between two people includes at least four dimensions: the way you see yourself, the way you see your friend, the way your friend sees himself or herself, and the way your friend sees you. Added to these, however, are two more complicated dimensions: the way you believe your friend sees you, and the way your friend believes you see him or her.

Given these dimensions, it should not surprise you if you and your friend have different perspectives on the same events. In light of these differences, you may wish to consider your friend's perceptions as subjective. On the other hand, you would be wise not to discount completely your friend's point of view.

Complete this exercise by doing something with your friend that reminds you of something you used to do together years ago. Play touch football, listen to old records, go to the neighborhood mall, make dinner together, or pursue any other activities that help you both feel consciously connected to the ''inner past'' you share.

DAY 6

BABES IN
TOYLAND

Today's exercise should provide you with an entertaining and emotionally positive sense of closure for the early memory exercises you've been practicing throughout Week One. Begin by visiting a toy store and spending about thirty to sixty minutes walking through the aisles. As you study the shelves, notice how many toys and games from your childhood are still sold today. From Barbie dolls (with all the outfits) to Monopoly and Mousetrap, from Etch-a-Sketch to Play-Doh, you'll be surprised at how many old favorites are still around.

If possible, go to a large toy department store, where selections are numerous and the sales help leaves you alone. You might find it difficult to browse through a posh toy boutique for an hour without salespeople giving you funny looks. But at stores like Toys ''R'' Us, where the large number of customers provides you with the mantle of anonymity, you can wander around forever—or at least until closing time—and no one will interrupt you or even particularly notice your presence.

As you walk around the store during the initial phase of this exercise, pay particular attention to any toys, games, or other items that are identical, or at least similar, to those you played with as a child. It is quite likely that just encountering these items will trigger powerful emotions and memories related to your childhood. Whenever you come across familiar toys or games in the store, imagine that you are playing with these objects right now. If you see a Barbie doll much like the one you had as a small child, imagine constructing an entire life for her in your imagination, just as you did as a child. If you see the board game Stratego, imagine constructing strategies for victory, just as you did when you were young. If you can handle the toy, do so. Think about the toy or game increasingly deeply—without being analytical—until, in your imagination at least, you are playing with it just as intensively as you did when you were young.

As you walk around the store, remember other toys that you may have used as a child, but which no longer seem to be around. Notice, also, any items you may have longed for as a child but, for whatever reason, did not have. Are there certain toys, games, or other items now in the store that the child you used to be would have especially enjoyed? What would it have been like to play with those objects? See yourself playing with those objects now. Take your time, and allow your emotions to emerge and carry you back in your imagination to your memories of the way you viewed yourself and the world as a child.

Complete this exercise by giving a gift to the childhood part of yourself. Was there some toy you wanted as a child but couldn't have? Do you recall a treasured childhood possession you lost long ago? Take this opportunity to buy yourself that gift you've secretly always wanted, or to replace that favorite possession.

Some people have found this to be a healing experience. As a twelve-year-old child, for instance, one friend of ours had been forced to stand and watch while his emotionally disturbed father deliberately crushed a beloved collection of plastic models. It had taken our friend years to save for and purchase the models, and he'd spent months building and painting them by hand. Thirty years later, our friend enjoyed a wonderful two-week vacation buying, building, and painting the models his father had destroyed.

DAY 7

THE TURNING
POINT

Among the most significant places in your life are those that symbolize a turning point—when you rejected one major personal choice or direction in favor of another. This symbolic location can be one in which you once escaped death, experienced personal tragedy or triumph, or made a dramatic, life-changing decision. To conclude Week One of the Total-Recall Program, therefore, you will focus on such a place, perhaps achieving a greater sense of your personal destiny in the process.

Begin today's exercise by returning to some psychologically significant site, representing a point at which you took one life path instead of another. (If you cannot physically return to such a site, substitute a similar spot to which you do have easy access.)

Once you arrive at your chosen spot, find a comfortable place to sit, relax, and focus on the surroundings. Allow your visual and other sensory impressions to carry you back to the major life event you associate with this locale. Recall, in vivid detail, what these surroundings looked like during that earlier period. Tap into your innermost feelings and recall the events and people crucial to your life at that time. Don't just analyze your feelings or review them from a detached distance. Instead, allow yourself to reexperience the past on as deep an emotional level as is comfortable and possible for you now.

After you reexperience your past emotions, reflect on how events in your life have since evolved. Then, just as you did on Day 3, imagine communicating directly with your own past self and sharing the knowledge and wisdom of your accumulated life experience.

Finally, try to achieve some sense of emotional detachment from the turning point upon which you are focusing. Then focus on the sequence of events that has unfolded from the time of the turning point to the present point in your life. How did the decisions you made back then lead to your current situation? What aspects of your life might be different now had you taken an alternative path?

Conclude this exercise by mentally conjuring the images of your past, future, and present selves all at once. Then allow these images to dissolve in a mental mist. As they fade from your conscious awareness, walk away from the symbolic spot you have chosen and psychologically leave it behind. Focus on your present self and on future turning points to come.

> ***Mental Note***—You may also practice this exercise with a partner, especially if the two of you have shared a turning point in your life. One couple, for example, practiced this exercise together following the San Francisco earthquake of October 1989. Shortly before the earthquake occurred, they had nearly signed a lease on a spacious apartment in the Marina district with a beautiful view of the Golden Gate Bridge. One of them believed, however, that the building would not withstand a major earthquake, and therefore convinced the other to take a more expensive apartment built on bedrock a short distance away. When the earthquake struck a month later, the first building collapsed and burned in a deadly inferno that made headlines in newspapers and magazines all over the country. The couple later stood at the edge of the smoldering ashes, feeling grateful for having narrowly escaped this tragedy. They experienced a deepened sense of appreciation for each other and for the extra time they felt they had both been given to make positive contributions in their lives.

WEEK ONE THE REMEMBERED SELF

DAY 1 WOMB WITH A VIEW	DAY 2 FETAL ATTRACTION
Learn about the specific details of your own birth.

Choose a time when you may relax in a warm bathtub in the dark without being disturbed for at least 30 minutes.

Before getting into the water, turn on a radio at low volume between stations.

Get into the tub, take a deep breath, and get comfortable.

Allow any thoughts or concerns about your present existence to drift from your mind.

Focus only on your physical sensations and the sound of the static in the background.

Consider the experience of your own prenatal development and birth.

Lift yourself out of the water, dry yourself off, and turn on a light.

Find a warm and comfortable place to wrap yourself up in a sheet or blanket for at least 20 minutes.

Reflect upon and fully absorb the impact of this experience. | Spend 20 to 30 minutes looking through a book of photographs showing the developmental progress of the human fetus.

Imagine that you are gazing at images of your own prenatal development, and notice the impact this may have on your emotions.

Lie down, get comfortable, and play a classical record or tape that is at least 30 minutes long. Focus on your memories of the photographs at which you looked earlier.

Relax, allow your thoughts to flow with the music, and remember any feelings the photographs inspired.

Close your eyes and imagine that the music is carrying you back to the womb. |

WEEK ONE THE REMEMBERED SELF (continued)

DAY 3 THE EYES OF A CHILD	DAY 4 PHOTO REPLAY

DAY 3 — THE EYES OF A CHILD

Choose a meaningful spot where you spent at least one particularly thoughtful occasion alone as a child.

Go to the spot, choose a substitute site that reminds you of the original, or sit alone in a quiet and dimly lit environment and visit the place in your imagination.

Take a deep breath, relax, and recall how you felt when you first visited this place as a child. Allow yourself to relive mentally your childhood experience as much as possible.

Imagine that time as we normally think of it does not exist, and that you can communicate directly with your childhood self.

DAY 4 — PHOTO REPLAY

Gather together as many photographs as you can from your childhood and young adult life.

Find a private and comfortable spot at home where you can relax without being disturbed while looking at your face in a mirror.

Place the photographs in a pile before you.

Take a deep breath and relax.

Gaze at the reflection of your face in the mirror and let your thoughts drift over the present-day circumstances of your life.

Consider any ways in which your feelings toward your present life circumstances may seem to hail back to the emotional ambience of your childhood or teenage years.

Spend at least 30 to 60 minutes reviewing the photographs you've gathered in a random fashion and occasionally glancing at your reflection in the mirror.

Pay special attention to any feelings of nostalgia generated by reviewing the photographs. Especially note specific memories triggered by—but not directly depicted in—the photos at hand.

DAY 5
THOSE WERE
THE DAYS

Notice the emotions triggered in response to these memories and relate these to any sense you may have of yourself in your present-day life.

Put the photographs away and make a conscious effort to let go of your feelings about the past for the time being.

Go for a walk or enjoy some similar, easy going activity.

Get in touch with a friend with whom you've had a relationship since you were a child or young adult. If such a friend is unavailable, choose someone who is available and who has known you for as long as possible

Get together with your old friend in person in or near the place where you and your friend first met, or conduct this exercise in an extended telephone conversation or in some other location convenient to you both.

Ask your old friend to help remind you of the kind of

person you seemed to be back when the two of you first met.

Discuss details that you couldn't reveal to each other at the time, but which you would like to talk about now.

Notice any ways in which your friend's memories and perceptions of past experiences differ from your own.

Focus on the changes you've both experienced since you last met, as well as on those aspects of your personality that remain.

Do something with your friend that re-

minds you of something you used to do together years ago.

WEEK ONE THE REMEMBERED SELF (continued)

DAY 6 BABES IN TOYLAND	DAY 7 THE TURNING POINT

DAY 6 — BABES IN TOYLAND

Spend 30 to 60 minutes walking through the aisles of a large toy store.

Pay particular attention to any toys, games, or other items that are identical, or at least similar, to those with which you played as a child.

Imagine that you are playing with these objects right now just as intensively as you did when you were young.

Remember other toys that you may have used as a child, but which no longer seem to be around.

Notice, also, any items for which you may have longed as a child but which you, for whatever reason, did not have. See yourself playing with those objects now.

Allow your feelings to carry you back in your imagination to your memories of the way you viewed yourself and the world as a child.

Buy a gift for the childhood part of yourself.

DAY 7 — THE TURNING POINT

Return to some psychologically significant site that represents a point at which you took one life path instead of another.

If you cannot physically return to such a site, substitute a similar spot to which you do have easy access.

Find a comfortable place to sit at your chosen spot. Relax and focus on the surroundings.

Allow your visual and other sensory impressions to carry you back to the major life event you associate with this locale. Recall what these surroundings looked like during that earlier period.

Allow yourself to reexperience the past on as deep an emotional level as is comfortably possible.

Reflect on how events in your life have since evolved.

Imagine communicating directly with your own past self and sharing the knowledge and wisdom of your accumulated life experience.

Focus on the sequence of events that have unfolded from the time of the turning point to the present point in your life.

Mentally conjure images of your past,

present, and
future selves
all at once.

Allow these
images to dis-
solve in a
mental mist.

Walk away
from the sym-
bolic spot you
have chosen
and psycholog-
ically leave it
behind.

Focus on your
present self
and on turning
points to
come.

WEEK TWO

THE DOORS OF PERCEPTION

WEEK TWO

•

THE DOORS OF PERCEPTION

*I*n Week Two of the Total-Recall Program you'll turn your attention away from the longer-term memories upon which you've been focusing and toward the shorter-term memories that comprise your awareness of the everyday world. If you stop to think about it, you'll no doubt realize that your ongoing memories form the scaffolding upon which your long-term memories are based. Developing a more powerful everyday memory will not only improve the quality and depth of your long-term recollections, it will also empower you as you negotiate the world.

The key to a potent everyday memory is an increasingly effective perception of the world. And that, in essence, is your goal for Week Two. As you work your way through the next seven exercises, you will focus on honing the input of your senses one by one. First you will work on better absorbing visual information. Then you'll go on to hone your senses of hearing, smell, taste, and touch as well.

As you practice the exercises in Week Two, you'll discover that enhancing your memory means tuning in, on a more intense level, to the input of all your senses. As you do so, you should not only become a more effective observer, you should also find your memory of all the facets of everyday situations becoming increasingly clear.

DAY 8

MOVIE MADNESS

In order to remember accurately something you've experienced, you must *observe* the situation in the first place. On Day 8, therefore, you will learn to sharpen your powers of observation, thereby improving your ability to remember the ''minor'' details of your everyday life.

To practice today's and tomorrow's exercises, you'll need a video-cassette recorder and a television. (If you do not own either of these items, they are usually available for rental.) Begin today's exercise by visiting a store that rents videotapes of popular films. Rent a feature you have never seen before, but which you think you might enjoy. Then return home, relax, and watch the movie.

Mental Note—Read no further until you have returned home and watched the entire movie. As soon as you have finished watching the film, proceed to the paragraph below.

Since you are reading this paragraph, you have probably just watched a feature film. You may now complete the questionnaire below, relying on your memory and nothing more. Answer as many of these questions as possible, provided that they relate to your particular film:

1. What was the opening line of the film?
2. What was the lead male character wearing in the opening scene?
3. What was the lead female character wearing in the opening scene?
4. What was the setting of the opening scene?
5. What kind of car or other vehicle did the lead character drive?
6. What was the color of the car or vehicle described above?
7. Describe something that was eaten by the lead character.
8. How many animals appeared in the film?
9. How many people wore uniforms in the film?
10. Describe the furniture in the lead character's home or office.
11. How many languages were spoken in the film?
12. What was the weather in the opening scene?

13. What was the weather in the closing scene?
14. What was the lead male character wearing in the closing scene?
15. What was the lead female character wearing in the closing scene?
16. What was the first line said by a supporting female character?
17. What was the last line said by a supporting female character?
18. How many guns were fired in the film?
19. How many different outfits were worn by the lead character?
20. How many houseplants appeared in the film?
21. How many windows were in the lead character's home or office?
22. What was the first line said by a supporting male character?
23. What was the last line said by a supporting male character?
24. How many cities appeared in the film?
25. Repeat the most memorable line in the film verbatim.

Now that you have answered—or attempted to answer—these twenty-five questions, you may take a short break if you wish to do so. Then replay the videotape from the beginning and see how you did with your answers. How many questions did you answer correctly?

DAY 9

PLAY IT AGAIN, SAM

Now that you've had a chance to sharpen your powers of observation, it's time to practice the same exercise again with a different film. Once again, this film should be one you have not seen before.

This time, however, as you watch the film, consciously pay attention to the props, sets, and other details that are essential to the underlying mood and fabric of the story. Don't try to memorize these myriad details.

Rather, simply pay close attention to what you are watching. As you do so, you may find that many of the relevant details are absorbed into your unconscious memory with little effort.

After you have watched the entire movie, proceed to the questionnaire that follows. (No fair peeking or taking notes!) Then take a short break and replay the film to see how you did. Just to keep from being too predictable, some of the questions that follow will be familiar, but others will not:

1. What was the opening line of the film?
2. What was the lead male character wearing in the opening scene?
3. What was the lead female character wearing in the opening scene?
4. What was the setting of the opening scene?
5. How many cars or other vehicles appeared in the film?
6. What color were the lead character's eyes?
7. Describe everything that was eaten by the main character.
8. How many children appeared in the film?
9. How many naked people were there in the film?
10. What was the name of the street where the lead character lived?
11. How many taxicabs appeared in the film?
12. What was the weather in the opening scene?
13. What was the weather in the closing scene?
14. What was the lead male character wearing in the closing scene?
15. What was the lead female character wearing in the closing scene?
16. What was the first line said by a supporting female character?
17. What was the last line said by a supporting female character?
18. How many people were killed in the film?
19. How many different outfits were worn by the main supporting character?
20. How many kitchens appeared in the film?
21. How many meals were eaten in the lead character's home?
22. What was the first line said by a supporting male character?
23. What was the last line said by a supporting female character?

24. How many airplanes appeared in the film?
25. Repeat the most memorable line in the film verbatim.

When you have finished answering the above questions, go back and review the film to see how you did with your answers. If you are becoming a more effective observer, you should have improved your score—and your memory—the second time around.

> **Mental Note**—Regardless of the score you achieved on this exercise, you can still practice it from time to time in an effort to improve your powers of observation and your everyday memory skills. Simply ask a friend to make up some questions for you, or watch the film together and then ask each other a variety of questions immediately afterward.

> **Mental Note**—Now that a week has gone by since you first practiced the "Fetal Attraction" exercise presented on Day 2, you may wish to repeat it at some quiet time this evening.

DAY 10

NEEDLE'S EYE

On Day 10, you'll hone your powers of visual observation further still. Begin by visiting a department store or museum. You'll need to bring along a small drawing pad and a box of assorted colored pencils. Once you arrive at your chosen location, select some especially interesting store window or showcase exhibit that contains a variety of complex details and images.

Begin the exercise by taking time to appreciate the overall impact of the display. Notice its underlying aesthetic effect as well as the more blatant and obvious elements that seem to jump out at you. Observe each element of the display in relation to the elements around it. Focus on each object in turn, and as you do so, notice the parts of which that object is composed. How do these parts fit together to form the whole? Pay attention to the colors of the objects on display. Notice the way in which the lighting affects the way these colors appear.

Then focus on the less significant objects in the display you are observing. For instance, if you're observing a display of scarves, notice the pedestals and shelves on which the scarves sit. If you're observing dolls on a shelf, notice the price tags on the dolls and the screws that hold the shelves on the wall.

Notice the exact relationship of these minor objects to the major objects of the display. Notice the relationship between all the minor elements of the display you have chosen to observe. Pay attention to the colors of these less significant objects. How do lighting effects used within the display affect the overall appearance of these objects? Finally, observe the individual components of which these minor display objects are made.

Then notice any signs or words that are used within the display, including the size, style, and form of the individual letters that make up these words. Notice the placement of these signs and words in relation to the most significant and lesser objects included within the display.

Notice the backdrop of the display, including the colors of the surrounding walls, floor, and ceiling. If there is a mural or other picture painted on the walls, notice the relationship of any images depicted to the individual objects presented within the display.

Finally, move back a short distance from the display, and once again allow yourself to absorb the overall impact. Take a few moments to allow yourself to fully absorb this impact, then move away from the display entirely to a nearby spot from which it is no longer visible. Find a quiet place where you can sit and draw pictures on the pad you've brought along without being disturbed.

Your assignment, at this point, is to use the pad and the colored pencils to produce a drawing that depicts, as closely as possible, the entire display upon which you have just been focusing. For the purposes of this exercise, you need not create a magnificent and timeless work of art. Rather, you should simply produce a drawing that accurately represents your memory of the entire display. Using the colored pencils, you should be able to represent not only shape and location, but color as well. Take your time, and remember as many visual details of the display as possible.

As soon as you have completed your drawing, go back and check its accuracy against the real thing. Notice those aspects of your drawing that are precisely on target, as well as those that represent distorted memories of your original experience. You may be surprised to find that some of the details you felt certain about and confidently depicted in your drawing are inaccurate. On the other hand, details you only guessed at may be right on target.

To achieve the greatest potential benefit from this exercise, it is essential that you remember the *feelings* you had when accurately drawing various details of the display. Compare these with the feelings you had while drawing apparent recollections that turned out to be inaccurate.

Did your correct recollections emerge in a burst of spontaneous insight, for example, while your incorrect recollections seemed much more analytical? Or did your correct recollections seem to come pouring forth as quickly as you could put them down on paper, while your incorrect recollections came forth as easily as squeezing toothpaste from the bottom of an almost empty tube? By comparing your subjective sensations during correct versus incorrect memory impressions, you can actually learn to recognize which of your apparent memories of various experiences and events are most likely to be accurate, and which are not.

For this reason, you should not consider it a failure if you did not accurately recall all the details of the display you studied when the exercise began. Inaccurate recollections actually provide you with vital information that is essential to improving your memory.

Take a break, then repeat this entire exercise while focusing on a second display containing objects completely different from the first. For instance, if you observed scarves and hats before, you might observe a display of crystal vases or best-selling books.

As you carry out the drawing phase of the exercise, remember those feelings that you previously associated with correct versus incorrect recollections. Try to use this knowledge to your advantage.

Mental Note—By practicing this exercise from time to time, you should be able to improve your overall ability to remember visual details in your everyday life.

DAY 11

SOUND EFFECTS

On Day 11, you'll focus on developing your auditory memory. You may have noticed that your memory for certain sounds —a favorite tune you often play on your violin, the enthusiastic intonations of an especially important conversation, or even the sounds you associate with watching or participating in your favorite sport—remains clearer and more vivid than the corresponding visual memories. Today's exercise will help you further sharpen this vital aspect of your memory.

To carry out this exercise, you'll need two cassette-tape recorders, a blank cassette, and two or three prerecorded cassette tapes of instrumental music you have never heard before. The music itself can be any style you desire—from baroque to jazz to rock, provided there are no lyrics and provided the music is entirely original and not simply an adaptation of familiar tunes.

Begin by finding a comfortable place where you can relax without being disturbed or disturbing others. It is especially important that you not be disturbed by any outside sounds. You may wish to plug a set of headphones into your tape recorder for this purpose. Once you feel comfortable, pick out one of the prerecorded tapes and listen to approximately five minutes of music. (It is not necessary for you to time this portion of the exercise to the exact second.)

Begin the exercise by taking time to appreciate the overall impact of the music. Notice its underlying emotional effect and decide whether you find the selection aesthetically appealing. Notice those aspects of the music that immediately capture your attention—including specific sounds or instruments that are central to the composition as a whole. Notice, in particular, the underlying beat and rhythm of the tune you have chosen. Then notice the minor instruments that also provide essential components of the piece. Notice all the individual components of the music and the ways in which they intermingle to form the overall tune. Pay attention to the basic pattern of the music you are hearing, especially noting any repetitive features. Notice also any nonrepetitive, disturbing, or surprising elements in the composition.

Finally, allow yourself to appreciate once again the overall impact of the musical selection you have chosen. Take a few moments to fully absorb this impact, and quietly hum along with the music. Then, when you feel ready to do so, gradually lower the volume on your recorder until the music becomes inaudible and turn the recorder off.

For the next part of this exercise, place the blank cassette tape in the second recorder and switch on its recording function. Now, to the best of your ability, audibly hum or sing the tune you have just heard into the second tape recorder. Repeat as much of the tune as you can for the next five minutes. Then rewind both recorders and simultaneously replay both the prerecorded tape and the cassette you've just recorded. As you do so, check the accuracy of your recollection against the tune itself. Notice those aspects of your recollection that are precisely on target, as well as those that are not. Remember any feelings you had when recording accurate recollections and contrast these with the feelings you had when recording inaccurate recollections.

Take a break of at least thirty minutes, then repeat this entire exercise while focusing on a second, completely different piece of music. To maintain a fresh perspective, your second selection should involve different artists, different instruments, and a different style of music from the selection you heard earlier.

As you attempt to reproduce the selection on your tape recorder, remember those feelings that you previously associated with correct versus incorrect recollections and see if you can use this knowledge to your advantage.

> ***Mental Note***—Once you are successful at reproducing—or at least approximating—the tune you heard earlier, you may wish to take this exercise further by practicing with musical selections played for longer than five minutes.

> ***Mental Note***—With a little imagination, you can practice many variations on this basic auditory memory exercise. You may, for example, practice this exercise using videotapes of feature films. Play the tape and, with your eyes closed, listen to the music, sound effects, and dialogue. Then reproduce your auditory experience, as precisely as possible, on tape.

> ***Mental Note***—You may use similar techniques to recall sounds in your environment, from the chirping of birds to the noise of traffic. Try the technique during your morning commute to the office, for instance, or during a visit to the neighborhood park. By regularly honing your auditory memory skills, you should be able to improve your overall ability to remember a variety of auditory details in your everyday life.

DAY 12

THE NOSE
KNOWS

On Day 12, you'll focus your attention exclusively on honing your olfactory memory—that is, your memory for smells. To conduct today's exercise, you'll need to gather half a dozen perfumes

or colognes that you have never smelled before and that do not particularly remind you of the scents worn by anyone you know or have
known. (Small samples of new scents are usually available at the perfume and cologne counters in department stores.)

> **Mental Note**—Use either six perfumes or six colognes. Since perfume is,
> in general, so much more powerful than cologne, a perfume and a
> cologne would be too simple to differentiate for the purposes of this
> exercise.

> **Mental Note**—If you can't adequately practice this exercise because you
> have a cold, please save it for another day.

> **Mental Note**—If you're allergic to perfumes, please substitute any other
> olfactory sensation. You can, for instance, try this exercise with different
> types of cheeses, wines, or spices.

Once again, begin by finding a comfortable place where you can
relax without being disturbed. It is especially important for today's
exercise that you not be disturbed by any outside smells, such as the
smell of clean laundry or the aromas of home cooking drifting in from
a nearby kitchen.

Once you feel comfortable, pick out six perfume samples or six
cologne samples and place these unopened in front of you. Then take
one of the perfume or cologne samples and notice the brand name given
to it by the manufacturer. Finally, open the sample carefully, hold it
close to your nose and gently inhale the fragrance. Be especially careful
not to splash any of the liquid on yourself or on your clothes. (You can
also ask a friend to assist you by passing the individual samples under
your nose while your eyes remain closed throughout this entire session.)
Take a few moments to appreciate the overall impact and subtle qualities
of each scent. Then open your eyes, reseal the sample, and take a two-
minute break to clear your nasal passages before going on to the next
scent.

Repeat this exercise in turn with each of the half dozen perfume or
cologne samples you have chosen, taking a two-minute break between
each one to clear your olfactory sense of the previous scent. Once you
have completed this portion of the exercise, take a short break before
moving on.

For the next phase of the exercise, once more enlist the help of your
friend, if at all possible. Indeed, since you'll be trying to identify
individual scents through your sense of smell alone, it would be best

for you not to handle the individual sample bottles, which would no doubt provide you with other, nonolfactory clues. Your friend should simply pass the individual samples under your nose one at a time in a random order, giving you a few moments between each one to clear your senses before you smell the next sample.

As each opened sample is passed under your nose, try to identify the brand name associated with that particular scent. Ask your friend to tell you whether you are correct or incorrect only after you have attempted to identify all six samples. Of course, you are free to change your mind at any point and switch around your choices before you finally open your eyes.

Once again, notice those recollections that turned out to be precisely on target, as well as those that represented distorted memories of your original experience. Remember the feelings you associated with your accurate recollections and contrast these with the feelings accompanying inaccurate recollections.

Take a break of at least thirty minutes, then repeat this entire exercise while focusing on a completely different set of samples. If you used cologne the first time you practiced this exercise, you should now switch to perfume. If you used perfume, switch to cologne. This should help you to maintain a fresh perspective. As you try to identify scents from memory, tap into those feelings you associated with correct recollections and use this knowledge to your advantage.

Mental Note—Once you are successful at identifying the scents you sampled earlier, you may wish to take this exercise further by practicing with more than six samples of perfume or cologne at a time, or by allowing yourself increasing intervals between sampling the individual scents and trying to identify them later on.

Mental Note—You can practice many variations on this basic olfactory memory exercise. You may, for example, use such varied aromas as those associated with motor oil, fertilizer, blue cheese, floor wax, flowers, and spices. A word of caution: do not inhale any scents that the manufacturer warns against inhaling, or that might be harmful. Especially avoid glue of any kind, spray paint, car exhaust fumes, or asbestos.

Mental Note—As a further elaboration of this olfactory memory technique, you can attempt to recall scents associated with your spouse, the family pet, your home, your office, your favorite park, the ocean, or any other important person, place, or thing. You can even mentally "replay" the scents you encounter in the world around you as you go about your life, continually noticing and remembering the various aromas you come across every day.

DAY 13

CULINARY CONSCIOUSNESS

On Day 13, you'll focus your attention exclusively on developing your gustatory memory—your memory for tastes. The basic approach in this exercise will be similar to the one you've been using throughout much of Week Two. To carry out today's exercise, you'll need to gather two dozen liquid samples of unusual tastes you have not previously experienced. The easiest way to accomplish this objective is to visit a store, such as Cost Plus in San Francisco or Zabar's in New York City, that specializes in exotic foods and spices from all over the world. Pick out a dozen unusual liquid condiments that appear to be as different from one another as possible. You might, for example, choose a few different varieties of hot sauces based on different basic ingredients, a few salty selections, and some spicy, sweet, bitter, and sour choices. After you have made these selections, pick out a dozen more condiments that superficially appear to be quite similar to one another, but that are prepared by a variety of manufacturers who have introduced their own subtle variations in the ingredients. For this second group of condiments, you might choose half a dozen English steak sauces or mustards whose ingredients seem essentially similar with only minor variations, or varieties of Indian chutney with subtle differences in their contents. While you're at the store, you should also pick up a small box of plain unsalted crackers.

Return home with your selections and find a comfortable spot— preferably a table at which you can sit—and place the bottled condiments in front of you. You should also keep a pitcher of water, a glass, a stack of paper napkins, and the opened box of crackers handy. Open all the bottles of condiments, but leave the caps on loosely so that you won't be influenced by aromas that might otherwise leak out of the bottles. Then separate the bottles into the two distinct groups of condiments described above.

Begin the exercise by focusing on the first group of mixed condiments on the table before you. Take the first bottle and place a small sample on a cracker. Close your eyes, place the cracker in your mouth, and taste the contents of the cracker without swallowing it. Take a few moments to appreciate the overall impact and subtle qualities of the condiment you have chosen, including any underlying variations that may emerge from the contributions of various blended ingredients. Then open your eyes, spit everything out into one of the napkins, rinse out your mouth with a swallow of water, and take a three-minute break. Remember to reseal the first condiment bottle once your eyes are open.

> ***Mental Note***—You may, if you wish, ask a friend to assist you by pre-paring individual samples and passing them to you so that your eyes can remain closed, enabling you to focus exclusively on taste.

Repeat this exercise in turn with each of the half-dozen condiment samples in the first group, taking a three-minute break between each one to clear your palate of the previous taste. When you have completed this portion of the exercise, take another short break before proceeding to the next stage.

For the next phase of this exercise, you'll need to enlist a friend's assistance. Have your friend put individual samples of each condiment on crackers and hand them to you, in random order, one at a time. As before, wait about two minutes between each taste sensation. Try to identify the individual condiments you sampled earlier, relying on your sense of taste alone. Each time you identify a condiment, your friend should quietly note to himself or herself whether or not you're correct; however, your friend must not tell *you* how you've done until you've tasted all six samples.

Once again, notice those recollections that turned out to be precisely on target, as well as those that represented distorted memories of your original experience. Remember the feelings you associated with your accurate recollections and contrast these with the feelings that accompanied inaccurate recollections.

Take a break of at least thirty minutes, then repeat this exercise with the second set of condiment samples you collected. The second set of condiments will provide a more demanding challenge for your memory, because the differences between individual samples should be much more subtle.

As you work with the second set of condiments, remember those feelings you associated with correct versus incorrect recollections and see if you can use this knowledge to your advantage.

Mental Note—Once you have successfully identified the tastes you sampled earlier, you can carry this exercise further by practicing with more than six samples of various condiments, or by allowing yourself increasing intervals between sampling the individual tastes and trying to identify them later on. You may also practice this exercise with a wide variety of cheeses, various kinds of cooking oils, or a selection of wines. Of course, you should never ingest anything that might be harmful to your health or that violates any dietary restrictions to which you must adhere.

DAY 14

ONCE MORE, WITH FEELING

On the final day of Week Two, you'll hone your tactile memory—that is, your memory of your sense of touch. To carry out today's exercise, you'll need to enlist the cooperation of at least half a dozen relatively close friends who will not mind if you touch their faces. It would be best if there were both males and females in the group.

Gather your friends together where you can all sit comfortably within arm's reach of one another without being disturbed. The exercise should be done in total silence, and with as little fidgeting or moving around as possible.

Begin the exercise by visually signaling one of your friends that you are ready to start. Your friend should nod or make some similar visual signal when he or she is also ready for you to begin. With your eyes closed, slowly move one of your hands over and around all the features on your friend's face, paying detailed attention to its features, from the size and shape of the nose to the curve of the upper lip. The hand you use should be the opposite of the one you use to write. Notice the texture of your friend's skin—its general roughness or softness, its firmness or flexibility, its clear, smooth path or rough-hewn surface. Notice the texture and sensations associated with touching your friend's hair, the way in which your friend's face responds to your touch as you slowly go through these motions. Finally, open your eyes and notice the connections you make in your mind between the tactile sensations you have just experienced and your close-up visual experience of your friend's facial features.

Repeat this exercise in turn with each of the half dozen friends you have gathered, opening your eyes and taking a two-minute break between each tactile exploration. When you have completed this portion of the exercise, take another short break before proceeding to the next stage.

For the next phase of this exercise, your friends should momentarily leave the room. After they have left, once more close your eyes. Your friends should then return as silently as possible and surround you, sitting in different positions from where they were before.

With your eyes remaining tightly shut until this phase of the exercise is completed, you should once again slowly move your hand over each of your friends' faces. Pay attention to the details of their features and attempt to identify each individual in turn, relying solely on your sense of touch. After you feel you have identified a person, call out the name. Your friends should inform you as to the accuracy of your results only after you have gone through the whole group and opened your eyes. After you hear the results, think back to the recollections that turned out to be precisely on target, as well as those that represented distorted memories of your original experience. Remember the feelings associated with accurate and inaccurate recollections and use these to help you remember tactile sensations in the future.

Mental Note—In the spirit of fair play and friendly social interaction, each of your friends should get a chance to try the tactile memory exercise as well.

Mental Note—You may practice a second round of the tactile exercise with the same friends, or with an entirely different set of friends, if they are available. You may also try this exercise using your other hand to see if this makes a difference.

Mental Note—You can practice many variations on this basic tactile memory exercise by using different types of leaves (a variety of evergreen branches would be ideal for this exercise) or even by working with a variety of toy action figures or plastic dinosaurs. One of our friends actually created an exercise based on a variety of whole, fresh fish from her local market.

Congratulations! You've just completed Week Two of the Total-Recall Program.

WEEK TWO THE DOORS OF PERCEPTION

DAY 8 MOVIE MADNESS	*DAY 9* PLAY IT AGAIN, SAM	*DAY 10* NEEDLE'S EYE	
Make sure you have a video-cassette re-corder and a television. Rent a feature film on video-tape. Complete the questionnaire. Take a break. Replay the tape to see how many questions you answered cor-rectly.	Repeat yester-day's exercise with a different film. This time, however, as you watch the film pay atten-tion to the props, sets, and other de-tails that are essential to the underlying mood and fab-ric of the story. After you have watched the entire movie, answer the questionnaire. Take a short break and re-play the film to see how you did.	Visit a depart-ment store or museum. Bring along a small drawing pad and a box of assorted col-ored pencils. Select and then observe an in-teresting show-case. Find a quiet place where you can sit and draw pictures without being disturbed. Depict the en-tire display as closely as pos-sible. As soon as you have com-pleted your drawing, go back and check its accuracy against the real thing. Remember the *feelings* you had when ac-curately draw-ing the	display. Com-pare these with the feelings you had while drawing appar-ent recollec-tions that turned out to be inaccurate. Take a break, then repeat the exercise while focusing on a second display containing objects completely dif-ferent from the first. As you carry out the drawing phase of this exer-cise, remember those feelings that you previ-ously associ-ated with correct versus incorrect recol-lections. Try to use this knowl-edge to your advantage.

DAY 11
SOUND
EFFECTS

DAY 12
THE NOSE
KNOWS

Prepare two cassette-tape recorders, a blank cassette, and two or three prerecorded cassette tapes of instrumental music you have never heard before.

Find a comfortable place where you can relax without being disturbed or disturbing others.

Listen to the music. Notice all the individual components of the music and the ways in which they intermingle to form the overall tune.

Quietly hum along with the music. Gradually lower the volume on your recorder until the music becomes inaudible and turn the recorder off.

Place a blank cassette tape in the second recorder and switch on its recording function. Audibly hum or sing the tune you have just heard into the second tape recorder. Repeat as much of the tune as you can for the next five minutes. Then rewind both recorders and simultaneously replay both the prerecorded tape and the cassette you've just recorded. As you do so, check the accuracy of your recollection against the tune itself.

Remember any feelings you had when recording accu-

rate recollections and contrast these with the feelings you had when recording inaccurate recollections.

Take a break of at least 30 minutes, then repeat this entire exercise while focusing on a second, completely different piece of music. Remember those feelings that you previously associated with correct versus incorrect recollections and see if you can use this knowledge to your advantage.

Gather half a dozen perfumes or colognes that you have never smelled before and that do not particularly remind you of the scents worn by anyone you know or have known.

Find a comfortable place where you can relax without being disturbed.

Place the selected samples unopened in front of you. Inhale each scent, in turn, with a two-minute break in between each sample.

Take a short break.

Have a friend pass each sam-

(continued)

WEEK TWO THE DOORS OF PERCEPTION (continued)

DAY 12 THE NOSE KNOWS	DAY 13 CULINARY CONSCIOUSNESS

ple under your nose—in random order—and see if you can identify it.

Notice those recollections that turned out to be on target, as well as those that represented distorted memories of your original experience. Remember the feelings you associated with your accurate recollections and contrast these with the feelings accompanying inaccurate recollections.

Take a 30-minute break, then repeat the exercise, focusing on a completely different set of samples. As you try to identify scents from memory, tap into those feelings you associated with correct recollections and use this knowledge to your advantage.

Gather two dozen samples of unusual tastes you have not previously experienced and a small box of plain unsalted crackers.

Prepare a pitcher of water, a glass, a stack of paper napkins, and the opened box of crackers.

Separate the bottles into the two groups— one in which tastes are widely varying, and one in which tastes are similar to one another— and taste the samples, one at a time.

Take a few moments to appreciate the overall impact and subtle qualities of the

first condiment. Then open your eyes, spit everything out into one of the napkins, rinse out your mouth with a swallow of water and take a three-minute break.

Repeat with each of the half dozen condiment samples in the first group.

Take a short break.

Have a friend put individual samples of each condiment on crackers and hand them to you, in random order, one at a time. Identify the individual condiments you sampled earlier, relying on your sense of taste alone.

DAY 14
ONCE MORE, WITH FEELING

Take a break of at least 30 minutes.

Repeat this exercise with the second set of condiment samples collected.

Gather a group of your friends.

Sit comfortably within arm's reach of one another.

Visually signal one of your friends that you are ready to start. Wait for your friend's return signal of readiness.

Close your eyes and slowly move your hand over and around all the features on your friend's face. Use the opposite hand from the one you use to write.

Open your eyes and notice the connection between the tactile sensations and your close-up visual experience.

Repeat this exercise in turn with each of the half dozen friends you have gathered.

Take a short break.

Have your friends leave the room.

Close your eyes, and have your friends return one at a time.

Once more move your hand over each face in turn, and try to identify the person solely through your sense of touch.

After you feel you have identified a person, call out his or her name. Your friends should inform you as to the accuracy of your results af-

ter you have gone through the whole group and opened your eyes.

After you hear the results, think back to the recollections that turned out to be precisely on target, as well as those that represented distorted memories of your original experience. Remember the feelings associated with accurate and inaccurate recollections and use these to help you remember tactile sensations in the future.

WEEK THREE

RIGHT-BRAIN MEMORY

WEEK THREE

•

R I G H T - B R A I N
M E M O R Y

Whenever you find yourself struggling to recall a name, remember a conversation, or place a face, you can be sure the information is *somewhere* in the rolling, steamy outback of your unconscious mind. The unconscious mind— sometimes referred to as the "right brain" by experts who differentiate it from the more linear and analytically oriented "left brain" is believed to be home to virtually every significant fact you have managed to repress or consciously forget. (While the "right brain" and "left brain" are not necessarily directly associated with the right and left hemispheres of the physical brain, these terms are still used to distinguish between the analytic and nonanalytic aspects of cognitive functioning.)

In Week Three of the Total-Recall Program you will learn to navigate the sensitive and evocative realm of the right brain. As you do so, you will enhance your memory by tapping the powers of your insightful but often-repressed unconscious mind. To start the process, you will explore your unconscious mind by recalling your dreams. As you become more intimately acquainted with the realm of dreams, the innermost terrain of your unconscious will be revealed. As you come in closer contact with your unconscious inner self, you should be better able to navigate its byways, extracting information—in the form of memories—whenever you need it.

Week Three will help you explore your right brain in other ways as well. In one exercise, for instance, you will learn to achieve the state of alert relaxation, in which your body becomes deeply relaxed while your mind remains acutely alert. While you are in this altered state of consciousness, right-brain memories should more easily emerge. You will also tap memories buried in your unconscious through the technique of "emptying," in which you clear your mind of all extraneous clutter, and through the technique of visualization, in which you re-create events as vividly as possible in your mind's eye.

In short, Week Three of the Total-Recall Program should enable you to touch base with information that is simply "stuck" inside your head, and with memories that have long been hidden from conscious view.

DAY 15

DREAM RECALL

In order to enhance your memory, it's important that you learn to focus not only on your waking life, but also on your dreams. By recalling the details of your dreams, you will, first of all, come to remember—and perhaps understand—a whole different realm of your existence. You will also establish direct conscious entree into the realm of the unconscious. Once you can recall the creations of your unconscious mind regularly, you will tune into details of your waking existence with far more clarity and insight. As you come to understand events based not only on the hubbub of happenstance, but also on the essence of your inner self, you should recall even the tiniest details in a far more lucid way.

> **Mental Note**—On Day 15, you will focus on recalling your dreams. Next week you'll take your dream work further with what dream researchers call "dream incubation." Dream incubation allows you to consciously influence the subject matter of your dreams by intentionally focusing on certain thoughts and images just prior to falling asleep. By focusing on the topic you are trying to recall, then dreaming about it at night, you may enhance the way in which your unconscious mind processes the material at hand.

> **Mental Note**—Because some preparation is required, please read through all the instructions for Day 15 before you begin.

The first step in any program of dream recall is setting up a dream diary. Your personal dream diary should be a notebook that you can store under your pillow or carry around during the day. Thus, we suggest an easy-to-carry spiral memo pad; if you run out of space on this pad, you can easily purchase another that looks essentially the same. While you're selecting a notebook for your dream diary, you should also select a special pen. We suggest an easily flowing felt-tip pen that will enable you to write while lying down. The pen used for writing in your dream diary should not be used for anything else. You may also find it helpful to attach a penlight to your dream diary, in case you find yourself waking up and remembering a dream in the middle of the night. Take the notebook you've chosen home with you before writing in it, and place it, along with the pen and penlight, under the pillow on your bed. Then say to yourself, *This is where I'll be recording my dreams*. Leave the notebook under your pillow until you're ready to go to bed.

Once you've set up your dream diary, go about the rest of your day. As you travel to work, shop at the supermarket, or take your kids to the park, observe the people around you and repeat these words silently to yourself, *Everybody has dreams*. Consider the meaning of this phrase and try to imagine what the various people around you might have dreamed about last night. Glimpsing your immediate surroundings, ask yourself what those around you might dream about tonight. What might *you* dream about tonight?

Then, quietly say to yourself, *From now on, I'll remember my dreams*. As soon as you acknowledge your willingness to remember your dreams, let go of the idea and forget about it for the rest of the day.

Later, after you've gone to bed, reaffirm your willingness to remember your dreams. Once again, let go of this thought at the moment that you acknowledge it, and avoid putting any psychological pressure on yourself. Then fall asleep.

To retain your dreams as completely as possible upon waking, you must first understand that dream memories can be as fleeting as your next breath of air. Therefore, whenever you start to wake up, whether in the middle of the night or the first thing in the morning, do not open your eyes or even move. Instead, take a while to stop and reflect on your past night's dream experiences. It is very important that during your first waking moments you focus entirely on recalling your dreams.

For this reason, it's best to arrange your sleeping environment to avoid even the tiniest distractions. If you usually sleep with or near another person, ask him or her not to disturb you before you get out of bed in the morning. If you usually wake up with the aid of an alarm clock, we suggest going to sleep early enough the previous evening so that you'll be likely to wake up long before the alarm would normally go off. (If you absolutely can't do without an alarm, set your clock radio to wake you up with soft, classical music.)

As you engage in dream recollection, don't pressure yourself to remember detailed and convoluted descriptions in exact chronological order. As you probably have found when trying to recapture other memories—such as the title of some forgotten song—dream memories are best approached with subtlety and grace. They must be allowed to steep—to emerge gradually and spontaneously into your conscious waking awareness.

You are most likely to remember details or fragments of your most recent dream upon first awakening. The thoughts, feelings, and images pertaining to this dream can often gently be followed in reverse order to gradually guide you back toward subtle recollections of your earlier dream experiences.

Recollections of earlier dreams, however, are typically as fragile as soap bubbles floating on the wind; they consititute the most subtle feelings and images gently blowing through the hidden passages of your unconscious mind. Any sudden movement in your thoughts, any momentary distraction, any attempt to force the memory can burst the bubbles and cause the images to evaporate before they appear in your waking awareness.

Remember, you must relax and, most important, give yourself time to remember your dreams. If dream images don't instantly float to the surface of your conscious awareness, just lie still for a while, keep your thoughts clear, and see what happens.

To keep your dream journal, give each dream a title after you record it. Also make sure that you always record the date and approximate time of your dreams. For each particular day, keep track of which dreams you had earlier in the sleep cycle, and which you had later on. As you write, be sure to note the setting or settings within which each dream occurred, the characters who populated the dream, any significant props or symbols that stand out in your mind, and any thoughts and feelings that the dream may have triggered. We also strongly recommend that you use your dream journal to explore the relationship between your daily concerns and activities and your dreams. Leave one or two blank pages after each dream entry so that you can add any additional thoughts or recollections that may occur to you as time goes on. Finally, when you record the images and symbols that comprise your dreams, make an effort to interpret their special meaning to you. Although it is not mandatory, feel free to draw any pictures that relate to your dreams; visual images can express the underlying meaning of your dreams in graphic form, or even trigger the release of deeper memories.

Mental Note—Get into the habit of writing down your dream descriptions just after waking up and before getting out of bed. The longer you wait, the more likely it is that these memories will fade or become distorted.

Mental Note—Remember to follow the dream-recall technique each morning immediately after you wake up.

DAY 16

BE HERE NOW

During Week Two, the individual exercises focused on one mode of sensory perception to the virtual exclusion of all the others. In today's exercise, however, you'll focus on becoming more consciously aware of all of your sensory experiences at once. Your goal is to develop a greater sense of contact with every aspect of your immediate world. As you become more fully aware of your everyday perceptual experiences, you'll be more likely to remember these experiences in the future.

Begin today's exercise by choosing an extremely quiet and secluded outdoor location. Ideally, the location you choose should be one with which you are unfamiliar. It should also include a comfortable spot in which you can safely—and we emphasize the word *safely*—relax. Some examples of suitable spots in which to practice this exercise include a sand dune on the outskirts of a populated area, a shady spot under a giant cactus in the desert, the deck of a ship out in the ocean, or a grassy spot in the middle of a park or forest. If the weather in your area is particularly unpleasant during the time you wish to conduct this exercise, you may choose a large indoor arena that is relatively empty. For instance, you might choose the college library lounge after midnight; the underground plazas and walkways of your city after rush hour; or the furniture section of your local department store during a quiet part of the shopping day.

Once you have chosen a suitable location, go there. Take at least fifteen minutes to walk around the general area and fully absorb the impact of your overall surroundings with all of your senses. Remember to use your visual and auditory senses, as well as your tactile and olfactory senses. Take in as many details on as many different levels as possible; feel free to use your general powers of observation as well as the specific sensory perception techniques introduced in Week Two.

After you have finished observing your surroundings, sit down in a comfortable spot. Take a deep breath and once more focus on the sensory impact of the area immediately available to your senses. Do not think about the future or the past, or about any of your current problems. Instead, try to let all that go and immerse yourself in the experience of your immediate environment, focusing on every detail from moment to moment. Focus on the details of each moment as it washes over you. When that moment ends, let it go and focus on the sensory details of the next moment instead. As Ram Dass would say, in other words, "Be here now."

If you are in a park or forest, for example, you might notice the graceful movement of a red-winged blackbird landing on a branch and disturbing the predictable pattern of a cluster of elm leaves growing just above your head. If you are sitting on the beach or on a sand dune, pay attention to the sparkle of the sunlight reflected in the grains of sand where you are sitting, and notice an ant crawling uphill with part of another ant's leg in its mouth. If you are looking over the railing on the deck of a ship, you might notice the repetitive patterns of ocean waves lapping around the bow, and a stream of air bubbles breaking on the surface while a giant sea turtle swims past you underwater. As you immerse yourself in your immediate surroundings moment by moment in this intense and focused way, you will most certainly observe countless tiny details you would have missed before.

What does all this have to do with improving your memory? Use the same techniques at a party with a crowd of people, and you should find yourself remembering faces, eye color, clothing, perfume, coffee-table books, and menus with far more precision than you ever have before. In fact, we feel confident that if you take the time and energy to carry out these instructions properly, you will remember the experience of practicing this exercise for years to come.

A good friend of ours practiced this exercise nearly twenty years ago off a secluded trail in an enormous pine forest. He says the memory of that experience is nearly as vivid today as it was that afternoon long ago. More recently, we had an opportunity to practice this exercise while sitting on the side of a cliff dozens of square miles from civilization in a wild desert canyon. Though the environment had seemed all but barren a few moments before, it suddenly burst to life with rattling snakes, hidden tarantulas, flying insects, legions of ants, scurrying lizards, tiny flowers, colorful rocks, and pointy clumps of vegetation; we could strongly detect the smell and feel of dry heat in the air. Merely thinking about that experience, which took place nearly two years ago, awakens memories of even the tiniest details of that glorious afternoon.

DAY 17

MEMORY MAPS

How do you know if your memories of recent events are accurate? Even if your own memories closely match those of other witnesses to those same events, there is still no absolute assurance that each of you is truly remembering things as they actually occurred. One way you can help to ensure the accuracy of your own recent memories is by reviewing the patterns of ongoing events in your head on a regular basis, in effect creating "memory maps" that you can later follow to get back in your mind to where you have been.

On Day 17, you'll learn to recall anything from the rules of driving to the progress of a conversation through intuitive memory maps. These visual memory maps may take many forms, depending on the situation at hand.

One friend of ours, for instance, created such a map to master parallel parking just minutes before her driving test. With only a few lessons under her belt, our friend had never been able to parallel park correctly, no matter how many times her instructor delineated the steps. Desperate to remember, she finally took a piece of paper and drew six small diagrams—each a step in the parallel parking procedure. She was able to study the diagrams for less than a minute before the driving inspector approached to take her out for the road test. When asked to parallel park, the six small pictures easily played back in her head. She parked perfectly for the first time ever, and was thrilled to pass her test.

We ourselves have also frequently used a diagramming technique known as "clustering" to recall the details of an important business meeting or conversation immediately after the event. The clustering technique allows you to impose your own, intuitive organization on any given sequence of events. By restructuring the episode so that it makes sense to you, you can increase your ability to recall many more details than you otherwise would. According to educator Gabriele Rico, the developer of clustering and author of the excellent book *Writing the Natural Way*, a cluster is simply a rapidly produced graphic representation of the patterns you perceive. Clusters allow you to juggle ideas so that one association begets the next. Even when you've done only your first cluster, therefore, you've activated your mind and are focused in a way that wouldn't have been possible if you had just sat down and said, "I want to remember the molecular evolution lecture I just heard," or, "I want to remember how to fix my car."

To create a memory map in the form of a visual diagram or cluster, you'll need a blank piece of paper, a pen or pencil, and, if you want to get fancy, about six felt-tip pens in different colors. To create a memory map after a detailed experience or event such as a party with a lot of social interaction, a lecture, or a meeting, sit by yourself for a few minutes and create a graphic representation of what occurred. Of course, no one can tell you how to visually depict complex instructions or interactions so that they make intuitive sense to you. Like our friend who mastered parallel parking, you may sketch whatever comes to mind.

However, if such diagrams don't come to you naturally—or simply don't emerge easily from the activity in which you've been involved —your picture should tap the clustering technique. To use this technique, simply write a word to define your topic in the middle of a piece of paper, then draw a circle around what you've written. If you're studying nuclear reactor design, for example, write down and circle the words "nuclear reactor design." Then let your thoughts roam freely and jot down any ideas and associations that come to mind. You may also draw quick and simple pictures to symbolize your concepts.

Place these words and pictures anywhere on the page that feels appropriate, circling them as you go along, and making no effort to deliberately organize them. You might, for example, find yourself writing down such things as "meltdown" or "nuclear fission." You might draw a picture of the reactor and its parts based on order of construction, say, or design concept. As you write, you should begin to discover that you know much more about reactor design than you previously thought.

When you run out of words and pictures, you'll find yourself with a graphic representation of the concepts you want to recall. At this point, you may use a pen or pencil—or colored pens, if you have them—to draw lines between the various circled words, connecting concepts that belong together in the same colors, and allowing the incipient patterns within your cluster to graphically emerge. You may, for example, use a red pen to connect those concepts that have to do with safety factors, and blue to connect words relating to the flow of water from one part of the reactor to the next.

The initial free-association process involved in creating the cluster soon becomes a self-organizing process and a pattern begins to emerge.

This pattern, which you have created yourself, should make more intuitive sense than the description your instructor supplied. It should also more easily stick in your memory for a longer period of time.

On Day 17, tap clustering and general memory mapping techniques as often as possible. Carry your pad and writing utensils with you throughout the day, and, whenever appropriate, take a few minutes to graphically depict anything you've seen or heard.

> ***Mental Note***—When possible, you can use the general memory map or specific clustering techniques while an event is in progress, even if you can't easily get away to write. Simply envision the map or picture in your mind's eye in as much detail as possible. And later, when you have some time, reproduce the map or cluster on paper as well.

> ***Mental Note***—Remember to practice dream recall techniques each morning right after you wake up.

DAY 18

REMEMBERING ON THE RIGHT SIDE OF THE BRAIN

Have you ever struggled to remember the name of a song you recently heard on the radio, or the name of someone you haven't seen in years? Most of us find ourselves tensing up in such situations, wrestling within ourselves to grab hold of some fleeting thought or image that will trigger a sudden recollection of the information we seek. The more we tense up, the less likely we are to remember the information. Yet the answers we seek often spontaneously pop into conscious awareness soon after we stop deliberately trying to remember them and instead focus our immediate attention on other tasks.

Such an experience recently happened to a friend of ours when a colleague called and asked him for the name and phone number of a woman he had met only briefly nine years before. Our friend remembered meeting the woman in question, but found it a brain-twisting task to try to remember her name. He promised to look her up in his "files," even though he knew those files existed only in his mind.

As soon as he hung up the phone, he stopped consciously focusing on the problem. Instead, he put aside ten minutes to relax while focusing his thoughts in an entirely different direction. He then continued to go about his business, resisting the temptation to focus on the woman in question. Within twenty minutes—while he was feeding his cat—the woman's name spontaneously popped into his mind. He immediately called directory assistance in her home state and obtained her phone number.

On Day 18, you'll practice a technique designed to help you achieve a similarly relaxed state of mind conducive to retrieving fleeting memories from deep within your unconscious. This centered state, referred to as "alert relaxation," is one in which you deeply relax your body while remaining mentally aware and acutely alert. Stress researchers and sports psychologists have found this state to be useful in relieving tension and increasing concentration. In our experience, achieving this special state also greatly facilitates the ability of the conscious mind to communicate with the innermost self, thereby stimulating the process of communication between the right and left modes of mental functioning.

To begin, sit in a comfortable chair, stretch your muscles, relax, and take a deep breath. Then tell yourself that you will make no effort whatsoever to recall specific people, places, or things while involved in the exercise below. Instead, you will simply open your mind so that memories may spontaneously emerge.

Now envision warm currents of mental energy slowly moving up through the soles of your feet toward your ankles. Feel the muscles in your feet gradually warming and relaxing as you imagine the currents passing through them. Imagine that the currents continue moving up through your calves, into your thighs, through your hips and buttocks, and into your lower back and abdomen. Proceed very slowly, giving yourself time for each group of muscles to begin relaxing before allowing the imaginary currents to move on to the next area of your body. Feel the muscles in your legs becoming heavy, warm, and relaxed, and sinking down into the chair beneath you.

When you feel your legs becoming deeply relaxed, imagine the currents moving in a clockwise motion around your abdomen, then up along your spine and through the front of your torso into your chest and shoulders. Feel the muscles in your stomach and lower back letting go of any tightness or tension as the current passes through them. Allow a feeling of well-being to flow through your body with the imaginary currents as you continue to relax.

When the lower half of your body feels relaxed, imagine the currents flowing upward through your ribs and shoulders—warming and relaxing the upper part of your body, leaving your back and chest feeling completely warm and free of any stress or tension. Imagine the currents turning around to move downward through your arms, toward your fingertips, swirling around through your fingers and hands, then moving upward once more and back through your arms and neck toward the top of your head.

Now feel the muscles in your neck and face gradually becoming warm and relaxed as the imaginary currents pass through them. Then imagine the currents flowing out through the top of your head, leaving your entire body feeling comfortably warm, heavy and relaxed, and sinking down into the chair beneath you.

Do not allow yourself to become so deeply relaxed that you'll find it hard to concentrate. Rather, you should focus on gently calming yourself and getting into a receptive state of mind for absorbing new ideas, while still remaining consciously aware of your surroundings. Remember, the key to success is learning to enter a state of deep physical relaxation while remaining mentally alert. If you should find yourself accidentally falling asleep while practicing this exercise don't worry about it. The moment you wake up and realize what happened just continue carrying out the exercise, without moving, from wherever you left off. At this point you'll probably already be quite relaxed, so the key will be to become even more deeply relaxed without once again falling asleep.

In order to maintain the desired state of alertness, you may find it helpful to imagine the warm currents passing through your body in a variety of changing colors and patterns. You may also find it helpful to practice this exercise only when you are feeling physically and emotionally rested and easily able to remain awake for the entire exercise.

Once you have achieved a deeply relaxed, mentally alert state, sustain it for anywhere from ten to thirty minutes, then return to a state of complete waking consciousness. To do so, wiggle your fingers and toes, slowly stretch your muscles, and then sit up.

To experience the greatest potential benefit from these instructions for achieving a state of alert relaxation, we recommend that you initially ask a friend to help guide you through the progressive relaxation exercise by slowly and quietly reading you the step-by-step instructions exactly as they're written above. You may also wish to make a tape recording of your friend reading you these instructions so that you can practice on your own after this initial session. Of course, if you prefer a more private approach, you can also tape record the instructions yourself. Once you've become practiced at achieving the desired state of mind and body, you'll probably be able to enter this state more and more quickly without needing to listen to anyone reading the instructions to you.

Remember, do not try to recall lost memories or the day's events while practicing alert relaxation. Instead, use the experience to calm your mind. You'll be surprised how many memories—including the specific memories you've been seeking—will gently wash back over you if you just follow the instructions above.

DAY 19

EMPTYING

As we discussed during Day 18, it is often possible to release hidden memories through deep relaxation. On Day 19 you'll carry this process one step further by deliberately emptying your conscious mind of outside distractions.

Mental Note—Before sitting down to do the emptying exercise, read the instructions for Day 19 in full.

To empty your mind of distractions so that the memory you seek can emerge, begin with a deep and measured form of breathing often called "centered breathing." To practice centered breathing, lie down on a carpeted or padded portion of your floor and close your eyes. Then enter a state of alert relaxation using the technique described in Day 18 above. After you have entered the alert-relaxed state, take a series of deep breaths from your diaphragm. Slowly breathe in and out through your mouth for five to ten minutes.

After you have become extremely relaxed, sit with your spine erect and continue to focus on your breathing. Feel the continuous presence of your breath as it rises and falls against your abdominal wall and moves millimeter by millimeter through your entire body. Breathe in as quietly and slowly as possible, so that if somebody passed a tiny thread in front of your nose, it wouldn't budge. Exhale even more slowly. Pause for a moment (or even hold your breath) between each inhalation and exhalation. This fixation on your breath will help minimize intrusive thoughts. Inevitably, some feelings, impressions, or physical sensations will invade, but let them float away in the movement and rhythm of your breathing.

> **Mental Note**—Do not hyperventilate. Also be cautious about this exercise if you suffer from emphysema, heart trouble, or similar conditions. Finally, if you are taking antipsychotic drugs, we suggest that you refrain from this exercise altogether.

Now close your eyes and focus on the sensation of purity and emptiness. You may also focus on breathing itself. If you would like a visual image to help you capture the sensation of emptiness, you may envision an unblemished snow field or an endless screen of soft white light. You may also imagine yourself inside of a large, glass-encased, water-filled snow dome (the sort of thing that often comes with an Eiffel Tower inside) with torrents of gentle snow falling all around. Let the emptiness wash over you for several minutes, clearing your mind.

Once your mind is completely empty and cleared of all distractions, you may gently tell yourself that some specific memory or item of information will come to you. But instead of immediately coming out of your alert-relaxed state, as you did on Day 18, this time you should sustain the state while keeping your mind as open and empty as possible. If you notice yourself holding on to any particular thought, simply let go of it the moment you realize what is happening and focus instead on a clear field of snow, a soft white light, or the inside of a snow dome (minus the Eiffel Tower, of course!). Maintain this state of mind for as long as you comfortably can, or until the information you need spontaneously pops into your mind.

> **Mental Note**—Even if the information you are trying to remember does not emerge in your conscious awareness during the emptying exercise, there is a strong possibility that it will spontaneously come to mind not long after you return to waking awareness. Once again, we suggest that you not deliberately struggle to pull this information out of your deepest thoughts but simply allow it to emerge while your conscious mind is occupied with other immediate concerns.

> **Mental Note**—You may use the emptying exercise to complement many of the exercises in the Total-Recall Program. Whenever maintaining a steady focus becomes a struggle, this technique should help you attain a more centered perspective.

DAY 20

MEMORY
ETCHING

On Day 20 you will learn to etch memories into your mind so that they may stay clear and sharp for weeks, months, and even years to come. To start the exercise for Day 20, spend an hour intensively interacting with a group of people outside your immediate family. The interaction may take virtually any form at all. You can, for instance, have lunch with some friends from the office, attend a church dance, spend Thanksgiving dinner with a group of cousins, meet with your weekly therapy group, or even visit the local pub.

No matter what form the interaction takes, approach it with the same style of focus and concentration that you applied during Day 16. Focus on as many details within as broad a range of sensory perception as possible, absorbing clues from the visual, auditory, olfactory, kinesthetic, gustatory, and tactile realms. Remember to focus on every moment as if it is all that exists—push everything but the present moment out of your mind.

Shortly after you have completed your hour of intensive interaction, find a private spot and use the clustering technique introduced on Day 17 to put the experience into a framework that makes intuitive sense to you. Then go about the rest of your day. At night, when you return home, retire to a private spot in your home and enter a state of alert relaxation using the techniques presented on Day 18.

After you have sustained a state of alert relaxation for about ten minutes, focus on emptying yourself of outside thought and stimulation as you did on Day 19. Let the emptiness wash over you for several minutes, clearing your mind.

Once your mind is cleared of distractions, recall the hour of intensive interaction you experienced earlier in the day. Let perceptions from all your senses rush over you. Maintaining your focused state of alert relaxation, go over each sight and sound, each taste and texture, exactly as perceived by you moment by moment. Let the event you experienced wash over you, with the full force of its detail and meaning, right now. If you have trouble sustaining your focus, empty your mind for a second by envisioning a blank white screen or a field of snow. Then once more focus on the episode at hand.

Let the details you experienced earlier in the day continue to etch themselves into your memory for at least thirty minutes. Then slowly open your eyes, wiggle you fingers and toes, and return to a state of complete waking consciousness.

Mental Note—Remember to practice dream-recollection techniques upon waking up each morning.

DAY 21

STATES OF GRACE

On Day 21, we'd like to introduce an advanced form of memory often applied by sport psychologists to help their star athletes perform with speed and finesse. The technique is similar to memory etching, except that instead of etching the memory of a conversation, personal interaction, or event into your mind, you'll etch the memory of some physical or manual activity that requires a degree of grace, precision, and skill. Using the "States of Grace" technique, you should be able to enhance your physical performance of such things as ice-skating, skiing, aerobic dancing, or auto repair.

To start the exercise for Day 21, spend thirty minutes or more practicing some enjoyable physical or manual activity: Put up some shelves, play tennis, or shoot some baskets at the park. When you have finished this activity, return home and find a quiet spot where you can have some privacy for at least an hour.

Once you have settled down, sit in a comfortable chair, stretch your muscles, relax, and take a deep breath. Then enter the state of alert relaxation. As you learned to do on Day 18, envision warm currents of mental energy slowly moving up through the soles of your feet toward your ankles. Feel the muscles in your feet gradually warming and relaxing as you imagine the currents passing through them. Imagine that the currents continue to move up through your calves, into your thighs, through your hips and buttocks, and into your lower back and abdomen—through your entire body. Proceed very slowly, giving yourself time for each group of muscles to begin relaxing before allowing the imaginary currents to move on to the next area of your body.

After you have entered a state of alert relaxation and sustained it for about fifteen minutes, empty yourself of outside thoughts and stimulation. Take a series of deep breaths from your diaphragm. Slowly breathe in and out through your mouth for five to ten minutes. Inevitably, some feelings, impressions, or physical sensations will invade, but let them float away in the movement and rhythm of your breathing. Focus on the sensation of purity and emptiness. If you want, envision an unblemished snow field, an endless screen of soft white light, or a large, glass-encased, water-filled snow dome with torrents of gentle snow falling all around. Let the emptiness wash over you for several minutes, clearing your mind.

Once your mind is cleared of distractions, recall the thirty minutes of physical exercise or manual labor in which you engaged before. Focus as much of your mental energy as possible on the memory of that activity, envisioning even the subtlest movements of each limb in your body. If, for instance, you practiced a figure eight while ice-skating, see yourself performing that figure eight with increasing perfection again and again. As you imagine the exercise, feel the tiny muscles in your body respond as if they were once more moving—even as you rest. Spend thirty minutes intensively reviewing your day's exercise in your mind.

Then, sometime before you go to bed, go out and once more engage in the activity you practiced earlier in the day. You may find—as do some of the world's best athletes—that your performance has dramatically improved.

> **Mental Note**—If you would like to improve your performance of some precision-oriented physical task, you should find the "States of Grace" exercise above especially helpful. As you continue to practice the technique every day, you should find that your muscle memory for your particular task becomes increasingly powerful and precise.

> **Mental Note**—Remember to practice dream-recollection techniques upon waking up each morning.

WEEK THREE   RIGHT-BRAIN MEMORY

DAY 15 DREAM RECALL		DAY 16 BE HERE NOW	DAY 17 MEMORY MAPS
Set up your dream diary and a special pen. Place the notebook and pen under your pillow. Go about your day, observe the people around you, and tell yourself that they all have dreams. Imagine what they will dream tonight. Vow to recall your dreams during the day. Vow to recall your dreams once more, before you fall asleep. Upon waking up, lay in bed quietly and let your dream memories come to you.	Record your dreams in your dream journal.	Choose an extremely quiet and secluded outdoor location. Walk around and absorb your surroundings with all of your senses. Totally immerse yourself in the experience from one second to the next.	Prepare a blank piece of paper, a pen or pencil, and, if you want, about six felt-tip pens of different colors. Have an experience. Sit by yourself for a few minutes and create a graphic representation of what occurred. If such diagrams don't come to you naturally—or don't emerge easily from the activity in which you've been involved—utilize the clustering technique. To use this technique, simply write a word to define your topic in the middle of a *(continued)*

WEEK THREE   RIGHT-BRAIN MEMORY (continued)

DAY 17 MEMORY MAPS	DAY 18 REMEMBERING ON THE RIGHT SIDE OF THE BRAIN	DAY 19 EMPTYING	
piece of paper, then draw a circle around what you've written. Then let your thoughts roam freely and jot down any ideas and associations that come to mind. Place these words and pictures anywhere on the page that feels appropriate, circling them as you go along. Use a pen or pencil— or colored pens, if you have them—to draw lines between the various circled words, connecting concepts that belong together in the same colors, and allowing the incipient patterns within your cluster to graphically emerge.	Sit in a comfortable chair, stretch your muscles, relax, and take a deep breath. Envision warm currents of mental energy moving through your body. Allow your entire body to become warm and relaxed. Maintain a deeply relaxed, mentally alert state for 10 to 30 minutes. Return to a state of complete waking consciousness.	Lie down on a carpeted or padded portion of your floor and close your eyes. Enter a state of alert relaxation. Take a series of deep breaths from your diaphragm for 5 to 10 minutes. After you have become extremely relaxed, sit with your spine erect and continue to focus on your breathing. Close your eyes and focus on the sensation of purity and emptiness. Once your mind is cleared of distractions, gently tell yourself that	some specific memory or item of information will come to you. Keep your thoughts as open and empty as possible.

DAY 20
MEMORY ETCHING

Spend an hour intensively interacting with a group of people outside your immediate family.

Focus on as many details within as broad a range of sensory perception as possible, absorbing clues from the visual, auditory, olfactory, kinesthetic, taste, and tactile realms.

Find a private spot and use the clustering technique to put the experience into a framework that makes intuitive sense to you.

Go about the rest of your day.

At night, when you return home, retire to a private spot in your home and enter a state of alert relaxation.

After you have sustained a state of alert relaxation for about 10 minutes, empty yourself of outside thought and stimulation.

Once your mind is cleared of distractions, recall the hour of intensive interaction you experienced earlier in the day.

Let the details of your experience continue to etch themselves on your brain for at least 30 minutes. Then return to a state of complete waking consciousness.

DAY 21
STATES OF
GRACE

Spend at least 30 minutes practicing some enjoyable physical or manual activity.

Enter a state of alert relaxation.

Empty yourself of outside thought and stimulation.

Recall the 30 minutes of physical exercise or manual labor in which you engaged. Focus as much of your mental energy as possible on the memory of that activity, envisioning even the subtlest movements of each and every limb in your body.

Sometime before you go to bed, go out and once more engage in the activity you practiced earlier in the day.

WEEK FOUR

TOTAL RECALL

WEEK FOUR

•

TOTAL RECALL

In Week Four of the Total-Recall Program you will once more visit the realm of the unconscious mind. Instead of merely inducing states of consciousness conducive to enhanced memory, however, you will examine the hidden patterns that form the infrastructure of your life. First you will examine your memories in search of these patterns, then you will learn to recognize the presence of these patterns in the details of your life. Once you have recognized global life patterns, you will use them to remember the true nature of events and relationships *as* they unfold. During the last part of the Total-Recall Program, you will also learn to collect memories; to sculpt new experiences as sources of meaningful memories in the future; and to generate memory implants, in which you invent make-believe memories to enhance your experience of life.

DAY 22

THE AMAZING TECHNICOLOR DREAMCOAT

On the first day of Week Three you learned a potent technique for recalling and recording your dreams. Today you will take your dream work one step further by searching your dreams for elusive memories you cannot, despite all your efforts, recall.

In order to search your dreams for hidden memories, you can practice a technique known as dream incubation, in which you intentionally induce a dream on a specific subject by focusing on that subject before falling asleep. When you deliberately induce dreams dealing with forgotten material, the material will be more likely to emerge.

The first part of the dream-incubation process for memory enhancement involves creating a relaxing sleep environment. Begin Day 22, therefore, by reflecting on the psychological atmosphere of your usual sleep surroundings. Consider the possible influence that any objects or images within this setting may have on your dreams. Are your immediate sleep surroundings rich in stimulating and nurturing images, such as works of art and pictures of your loved ones? Or is your bedroom sterile, marked by stark visual images and piles of work you've brought home from the office? Do you sleep and dream in quiet surroundings, or is the atmosphere frequently jarred by sounds of passing traffic or a television playing in another room? Is the usual temperature of your sleep environment comfortable? Is the ventilation adequate? Is the color of your room soothing to your spirit, or do you find it overstimulating or just plain boring? Most important: What messages do you receive from your sleep environment? What does it say about your personal relationships and values, and what does it reflect about your attitudes toward sleep and dreaming?

Once you have considered the issues above, make your dream room as calm and comfortable as possible. Decorate it with some favorite objects that express the most positive aspects of your personality. Do your best to make the room attractive, and remove any disturbing or intrusive images that might interfere with dream exploration.

After you have taken these preliminary and psychologically healthy steps, take a look around the room and consider some ways in which you may gently introduce certain aspects of the material you wish to remember. The idea is to introduce some subtle background stimuli that will nudge you toward a gentle recollection of the material you seek.

You might, for example, place a key near your dresser if you are trying to remember where you lost your keys. You might hang up a map of New York State if you're trying to remember in which town a potentially important New York contact lives. Once you've made your sleep environment conducive to dream incubation, it's time to focus on inducing a relevant dream. First, place your dream diary, special pen, and penlight in a prominent spot beside the bed. Then, as you prepare yourself for sleep tonight, focus on the information you hope to recall, gently excluding all other thoughts from your mind. Calmly tell yourself that you hope to find the forgotten information in your dream and, furthermore, that you hope to remember it upon waking.

Mental Note—You may further enhance your memory recollection by playing music specific to the particular material you want to recall. For instance, if you want to remember the name of a friend from high school, play music especially popular during your high-school days. If no musical style reminds you of the material at hand, you may wish to play some baroque music. At 60 to 70 beats per minute, baroque music moves at just about the same beat as the resting human heart. According to many psychologists, this form of music is particularly relaxing.

Finally, just before you turn off the light for the night and go to sleep, take a few moments to articulate (as best you can) the nature of the information you wish to recall. For instance, you might say, "I'd like to remember how to play 'Chopsticks' on the piano," or "I'd like to remember the location of the client list in my office." Then, using your special pen, write the phrase in your dream diary. As soon as you finish doing this, turn off the lights.

As you fall asleep, continue focusing on the phrase you've written in your dream diary and picture any relevant objects you may have placed around the room. Gently remind yourself to dream about the material you wish to recall. Remind yourself, also, that you will remember any relevant dreams when you wake up.

Mental Note—Keep in mind that you may not necessarily dream about the material you wish to remember in a direct way. Instead, your dream may include clues that you need to analyze or interpret—or at least focus on—if the memory is to emerge.

Mental Note—When you wake up, remember to practice the dream-recollection techniques you learned on Day 15. Before moving or opening your eyes, concentrate on your most recent dream experience. Follow these thoughts backward toward earlier images and impressions of the night's dreams. Record any dreams in your journal immediately after opening your eyes.

DAY 23

INNER
OLFACTION

The mystery had haunted him for years: Shortly after birth, salmon abandoned their snug river spawning ground and headed for the sea. But no matter how many leagues they traveled, no matter how many years they wandered, they always returned to their birthplace to spawn offspring of their own. To zoologist Arthur Hasler, the question was compelling: How did mere *fish* traverse such vastness of time and space to find their way home?

This question had plagued him in his lab at the University of Wisconsin, and pursued him throughout his years of service in World War II. Finally back home, in Utah, he took a hike in the hills one day and was hit by a rush of fragrant mountain air. Slowly, imperceptibly, the odor released his deepest memories, and for a moment he felt as though he were a boy again. He saw his friends traipsing up the slopes, heard their shouts ring out high and clear. In a matter of seconds the fragrance had carried him back twenty-five years. Then came a second rush of fragrance, releasing not a memory, but an idea. Hasler realized that salmon remembered the odor of their origins. They *smelled* their way home.

Today considered one of the grand old men of biology, Hasler spent much of his life proving his inspiration in the field, and his work has also influenced researchers investigating the human realm. Back in the days of the hunter-gatherers, researchers have shown, humans used olfaction not only to detect poisons, but also to choose their mates. In fact, today's scientists have mapped nerve pathways from the human nose to the limbic brain, the active center of memory, lust, and rage.

The detailed studies conducted by Hasler and dozens of others indicate the deep and abiding power of the sense of smell. On Day 23, you will become more consciously aware of the olfactory perceptions embedded in your deepest emotions and memories. As you relate your immediate olfactory perceptions to your long-term "smell memories," your ability to recall people, places, and things should improve. (As a bonus, Day 23 should help you fathom the occasional experience of déjà vu.)

Begin today's exercise by going to a department store that features large displays of perfumes and colognes. It would be particularly helpful if the store you choose has open displays of various scents readily available for its customers to sample.

Mental Note—If you are suffering from a cold, or any other respiratory disorder that might interfere with your sense of smell, postpone this exercise.

Mental Note—While we recommend using perfumes or colognes in this exercise, some people are allergic to these scents. If you fall into this category, please substitute any other olfactory sensation. You can, for instance, try this exercise at an open-air market that sells baked goods created on the premises, pickles in open barrels, or hot dogs and fries.

Once you have arrived at a suitable location, take a mental inventory of the scents available for sampling. Notice whether any of the perfumes or colognes (or other items) were used by a former lover, a close friend, a family member, or some other significant person from your past. Do you have any special memories of, or associations with, any of these scents in any way?

Once you have located some familiar brands of perfume or cologne, begin by choosing one that strikes you as particularly significant. If you cannot locate a familiar brand, just sample some unfamiliar scents until one strikes you as familiar. (Often, you may not know the name of a particular scent that was worn by someone in your past. You may also find a relatively new brand that has characteristics in common with a familiar scent.)

As you sniff your chosen sample, take care not to splash any of the liquid on your skin or clothes. Hold it close to your nose and gently inhale the fragrance. Take a few moments to fully appreciate the overall impact and subtle underlying qualities of the scent you have chosen, but do not focus on analyzing the scent, as you did on Day 12. Rather, close your eyes and let spontaneous images come rushing in. Immerse yourself in these images evoked by the scent as fully and emotionally as possible. Does the experience trigger an emotional flashback to another place and time? Does your mind fill with images of people and scenes from your past? Allow yourself to remember not only your present-day emotional responses to this experience, but also the kinds of feelings you had when the scent in question was part of your everyday existence.

When you feel ready, open your eyes, reseal the sample, and, if possible, try the same exercise with a second scent. If you use two scents, take a ten- to fifteen-minute break between each sample. After sampling each scent, allow your memory to wander over the feelings and images the scent has sparked. After you have finished your assignment in the store, find a quiet place to sit and ask yourself this: If you met a stranger wearing one of the scents in question, would your reaction be tempered by conscious or unconscious associations of the past?

As you go about the rest of the day, tune into the scents associated with the people, places, and things around you. As you tune into these scents, ask yourself whether any remind you of the past. If so, how? Let those old memories wash over you—and use them to remember the events of today. As you tune into these various smells, try to absorb them on a deep emotional level, so that they will be imprinted in your mind. The next time you encounter these odors, you should clearly remember the events of today. What's more, if you have a special need to recall the events of this day, you may try to do so by thinking of the associated smells. As you focus, in your mind, on the odors associated with today, whole images, feelings, and impressions should also come rushing back.

> **Mental Note**—If you like, you can conclude this exercise by purchasing an entirely new scent from the store. You may then have the pleasure of using this scent, at some point in the future, to trigger a memory of your life as it is today.

> **Mental Note**—Large numbers of olfactory sensations can send you reeling through memories of the past. The delicate aromas associated with institutionally prepared lasagne, for example, may take you back to the gourmet delights of childhood afternoons spent consuming the sacrificial offerings of your elementary school cafeteria. The smells from a local gourmet restaurant, on the other hand, may take you back to your mother's home cooking. And the smell of leather jackets and gin may remind you of your own first love, whose dream in life was to drive faster, talk meaner, suffer longer, and, in general, appear more intense than James Dean. As you travel through your everyday life, tune into the available olfactory stimulation and you'll be surprised at how often it is a high-speed freeway to the past.

The memory exercise above may be practiced with any of your senses. The sound of an old song playing in the background of a shopping mall or elevator, for instance, may trigger a feeling of nostalgia or even a sharp memory of what you were doing the first time you heard the song. The pasty flavor of a piece of flat bubble gum found in a pack of baseball cards may take you back to the newsstand where you once worked as a teenager. The feeling of cool silk against your bare skin may remind you of your earliest sexual experience. Even a tiny picture on a postage stamp or book of matches may remind you of some significant moment from your past. Remember, however, that the key is not only to focus on the memories you associate with various sensory perceptions, but also to take time to notice the relationship between such perceptions and your intuitive responses to events in the present day. In fact, the next time you experience déjà vu, you might stop and ask yourself if some inner part of you really is noticing an intensely familiar, but forgotten, aspect of the here and now.

Once you have begun to tune into your senses more fully, you will be able to use that ability to remember events unfolding in the present time. To do so, examine some of your spontaneous emotional responses to see if they are associated with any sensory impressions of your immediate environment. Then search your memory to see when and where that sensation first occurred. If you tap into an early memory you can use it later to remember the event unfolding today.

DAY 24

MEMORY
TRACKS

There are many ways in which the people you know and meet in your present-day life may remind you of those you've known in the past. Did your father have bushy eyebrows and wear a Budweiser tank top and boxer shorts around the house? Did your old girlfriend let her eyes go wide and wet every time she felt angry or hurt? Did your brother have the habit of pounding you on the back and laughing uproariously every time *he* told a joke? Your conscious and unconscious memories of such quaint idiosyncracies can easily influence your attitudes and behavior toward new people whose physical and behavioral characteristics remind you of the past.

Such memories need not even be especially blatant to trigger an unconscious association. In fact, you may find yourself intuitively liking or disliking, trusting or distrusting, attracted to or repulsed by people you first meet without quite knowing why. While many of these responses may prove to be on target, others can lead you to misjudge those you meet in your present-day life and to make decisions that are not always in your best interests.

Madison Avenue has long been aware of the ways in which such nonanalytic, emotional responses can influence our attitudes and behavior. Every day, millions of people are unconsciously stirred to buy products by models and actors capturing the essence of Mom and Dad, a fantasy lover, or a boss. Politicians, salespeople, and Hollywood producers use these tactics as well. One successful salesman we know, for example, had a special pair of eyeglasses made with nonprescription lenses to wear while pitching his wares. Although he has 20/20 vision, he believes that his customers associate glasses with intellectual credibility and fiscal reliability, and therefore respond more favorably to him when he is bespectacled than when he is not. He tells us that, in his experience, the technique actually appears to work.

By becoming more consciously aware of memories that influence your attitudes and behavior, you can gain increased control over your intuitive emotional responses, choosing those that are appropriate and rejecting those that are not. This will be your initial goal on Day 24.

Begin by finding a location where you can comfortably sit and observe the comings and goings of a wide variety of pedestrians from all walks of life. You might, for example, choose to practice this exercise at a bustling train station or airport, near a downtown street corner, or at a local tourist attraction frequented by visitors from all over the world. Once you have chosen an appropriate vantage point, sit quietly for at least thirty minutes and calmly observe the passing parade.

As you look on, consider the countless ways in which total strangers trigger recollections of people who have played significant roles in your past. Pay particular attention to the emotions that these complete strangers stir. Do you find yourself feeling automatically suspicious and angry toward someone who looks like your ex-wife's divorce attorney, for example, or favorably disposed toward an older woman in overalls and work boots who reminds you of the rugged and kindly grandmother who raised you on a farm in Kansas?

While such obvious reminders of the people in your past may be difficult to miss, stay on the lookout for less prominent physical and behavioral cues. An upturned nose, an oddly familiar facial expression, a regional accent, a certain color or style of hair, even a familiar first name can all trigger the unconscious mind; as a result, you might feel and act in ways more appropriate to the people of whom you are un-

consciously reminded than to the strangers you are encountering for the
first time.

As you continue today's exercise and become increasingly attuned
to the people around you, ask yourself if there are any qualities that
you can accurately predict based upon the unconscious cues to which
you are responding. At the same time, consider the ways in which these
cues might mislead you.

> **Mental Note**—You may discover that your ability to consciously draw on
> the intuitive wisdom of your memory can be greatly enhanced with prac-
> tice. If you tend to ignore this potentially valuable aspect of your aware-
> ness, however, you can expect it to fade more deeply into your innermost
> unconscious and thereby become less useful in your everyday life.

After you have examined the ways in which memory blasts from
the past influence your reactions, you may also wish to tap into these
same memories to recall what's going on in the here and now. During
the latter part of your day, go to a store, an outdoor plaza, a park, or
some other public place, and spend at least thirty minutes interacting
with—or just observing—the people around you. As you do so, compare these new faces to people from the past. For instance, when speak-
ing with that slim young man in the denim jacket, recall your old best
friend. Associating the conversation with memories of your friend
should impress it into your right brain more forcefully, enabling you
to recall specific conversational points at will. Later, when you get
home, see if your memories of the outing are more vivid and pronounced
than you believe they might otherwise have been.

DAY 25

GORILLAS IN THE
MIST

People virtually always provide you with early clues
to their true personalities, if you care to notice. Sometimes the clues
can be as overt as blowing pipe smoke in your face or asking to borrow
your apartment for an illicit affair. But sometimes the clues can be as

fleeting as a momentary change in facial expression that seems to be especially incisive or oddly out of sync.

On Day 25 you will learn to tune into such clues and commit them to memory. As you do so, you will not only become far more adept at remembering faces, you will also learn to use those memories to modify your reactions to people up the road.

Begin today's exercise by paying a visit to the ape and monkey exhibits at your local zoo. (If this is impossible, you may rent or purchase a videotape featuring primate behavior in the wild.) No matter how you conduct your observation, make sure you have a pad of paper and a pen or pencil by your side. Take at least one or two hours to observe carefully the behavior of these evolutionary antecedents. Pay close attention to the ways in which these primates interact with one another and, through your observations, try to make some judgments as to the basic personalities at play. While you're at it, ask yourself whether the behavior of any of the individual primates reminds you of anyone you have ever known. Now, before you leave the primate exhibit, take out your pad and pen or pencil and sketch a picture of the primate that has evoked the strongest response. Alongside that first sketch, sketch the human individual who most reminds you of that monkey or ape.

Once you have carried out this first phase of today's exercise, leave the primate exhibit (or simply turn off your VCR). Then go about the rest of your day. As you go about your business at work, at school, or with your children, study new acquaintances as well as old friends and colleagues much as you studied the primates. Look for facial and behavioral clues to their deeper drives and emotions, and, if possible, try to study these clues without interference from your more everyday associations.

Finally, tonight, sometime before you go to bed, take your sketch pad and sketch the people you observed earlier in the day. As you create your drawings, try to emphasize the facial expressions noted before. Next to each drawing, sketch a monkey or an ape with that same prominent expression or characteristic.

Not only should this exercise help clue you in to people's true nature, it should also help you to remember faces—and the intrinsic qualities that accompany them—with greater acuity than you did before.

DAY 26

INTUITIVE
MEMORY

At the end of Week One, we discussed the experience of a couple who narrowly avoided moving into a building that was later demolished by the 1989 San Francisco Bay Area earthquake. As you may recall, one member of the couple became concerned that the building would not withstand a major earthquake and refused to sign a lease on a beautiful apartment. Such a stroke of good fortune or intuition certainly looks impressive on a superficial level, and might almost lead you to believe in so-called "psychic" phenomena.

In reality, however, the concerned party had examined a map of San Francisco soil conditions several years before; the map had depicted those areas deemed especially unstable in earthquake conditions. Although our friend was not consciously thinking about the map when he went to look at the apartment—or even when he refused to sign the lease—he noticed a series of cracks in the building's lobby that triggered an overwhelming sense of danger when he thought about moving in. We consider it likely that these cracks were enough to alert his unconscious mind, which immediately cued in to the soil patterns he had seen depicted years before on the earthquake map. His unconscious—that is, his nonverbal right brain—responded with the appropriate emotion, a sense of danger.

It seems apparent from this and similar reports that the unconscious, or right brain, memory can frequently trigger uncannily accurate intuitive responses to a wide spectrum of situations. With practice, you should be able to use this memory to help you negotiate the world. What's more, as you tune in more strongly to the ongoing creation of right-brain memory, you should become increasingly able to retrieve it consciously, at will.

To begin today's exercise, take the same pad and pen or pencil that you used on Day 25 to a comfortable location where you can concentrate without being interrupted. On a blank piece of paper, write down a one-sentence description of some significant event in which, luckily for you, you decided to act based on a seemingly "irrational" instinct. For instance, you might write down, "Decided not to go camping and avoided being trapped in a forest fire," or "Predicted the stock market crash of 1987 and pulled all investments out of market in advance."

After you have chosen a phrase and written it down, take five or ten minutes to remember what was happening in your life just before the situation in question occurred. Especially recall the specific circumstances that led up to the unfolding of the event itself. Focus, also, on exactly how you felt just before the event in question took place. Were you in any way conscious of a rational reason for a problem to unfold?

After you have considered the questions above, take the pad and write your answers: For instance, you might write, "Was worried about the lack of rain in California," or "Noticed that the pattern of market fluctuations was similar to what happened just before the stock market crash of 1929."

Continue this memory exercise focusing on at least two more significant life events. Then, after you have completed today's exercise, consider the ways in which your memories of these past experiences have provided you with any insights into your own intuitive or right-brain memory processes that may be useful to you in future situations.

> **Mental Note**—Your right-brain memory or intuition can often alert you in advance to all manner of impending situations, but we suggest that you evaluate any apparent intuitive insights in the light of past experience and logic. While it is proper, in some cases, to take action based exclusively on your intuition, there are also many occasions in which it is equally appropriate to proceed cautiously while awaiting further information.

DAY 27

MEMORY BANKS

A few years ago a friend of ours visited her stepmother at her deathbed. The stepmother's husband (our friend's father) was deceased, as were all of the stepmother's blood relatives. In fact, the only people to visit the stepmother were our friend and her siblings—a group of people who despised the dying woman with a passion. But gazing around at the people above her, the sick woman, confused after months of drugs and illness, exclaimed, "Oh, what a happy family we all were."

Some people might have thought it a blessing that the stepmother died without recalling the family's pain, but our friend considered it tragic. After all, her stepmother had lived a passionate and tempestuous life. In the end, the memory of that life was all she really had—and she'd died bereft of that as well.

As Simon and Garfunkel observed in "Bookends," one of their famous songs of the 1960s, your memory is really "all that's left you." Of course, no one can preserve his or her memories in the face of mind-altering sickness and drugs. But even those of us who are healthy often pass through life in a whirl. Without stopping to consider events as they occur, the very essence of our lives—our memories—are often lost in a blur.

But there are some very simple and traditional memory preservation techniques to help you fight this tendency, and we suggest you tap them all. First of all, you can preserve your memories by keeping a journal. Your journal can take any form you like, though we suggest a simple, lined, spiral-bound notebook. Write in your journal daily if possible, and especially when you have something important to say.

You can also save your memories through the simple technique of collecting mementos for any occasion that is particularly important, happy, or profound. Did you spend a beautiful day at the beach with your new lover? Find and keep an irridescent shell to remind you of the day. Did your children love that vacation in Pennsylvania Dutch country? Buy a hex sign or other small token to remind you that you were there. Keep that matchbook commemorating your wedding or graduation day. Whenever an event is particularly significant, find a token to remind you that it happened and that you were there.

Don't forget to record memorable occasions on film and video. You may also use audiotape to record the voices of your loved ones, the sounds of special places and events, and the patterns of your thoughts.

We also recommend that you preserve your memories through music. Most of us are easily brought back to former times and places whenever we hear an evocative old song. Don't neglect to note the songs that form the background music to your life's epochs. In fact, you might buy some of these records and keep them around to stimulate your memories when you're in the mood.

In fact, we suggest that you make at least part of your residence a shrine to your memories, a place where you keep your old letters and personal journals, old pictures and mementos, videos and audiotapes. Remember, that beautiful day you spent with your spouse may be crystal clear right now—but that's exactly why now is the time to record it and set it in stone. "Preserve your memories, they're all that's left you." Start investing in your memory bank today.

DAY 28

MEMORY
SCULPTING

Before you begin today's exercise, we suggest that
you stop and consider the ephemeral nature of your journey through
life. No matter how intense any given moment may be, in fact, your
experience of that moment continues only until the moment has passed.
Indeed, a greater proportion of your life is spent in what has been your
past and what will become your future than in the here and now. What's
more, the way in which you handle the present will determine, to a
large degree, your impending future and your memories of the past.

With this in mind, we present the exercise for Day 28, in which
you will focus on creating optimum future memories in your day-to-
day life. Begin the first part of today's exercise by taking a mental
inventory of the memorabilia with which you currently surround yourself
in your home, office, or any other personally significant locale. Stop
and consider the ways in which many of the props that form the backdrop
of your daily life spontaneously trigger both conscious and subconscious
memories of the past. For instance, is your office paperweight a large
piece of slate retrieved during a camping trip with your old girlfriend,
who eventually left you for your best friend? Or do you use a wooden
cup from your Sweet Sixteen birthday at the Hawaii Kai—a fairly happy
event—to hold your paper clips? Such items of personal significance
not only have a way of triggering past memories, but can also continue
to influence your view of the present and the future as well.

Therefore, take the time now to inventory the memory environment
that surrounds you. Is your home filled with reminders of failed relationships, for example, such as the same polyester sheets with the
Flintstones pattern you had on your bed six romances back? Or is your
home filled with objects that make you feel good about who and what
you really are—a treasured bowling trophy, perhaps, or a college di-
ploma? Complete part one of today's exercise by removing any negative
objects from your everyday environment. We are not referring here to
such items as beloved photographs of deceased loved ones whose positive presence in your life is deeply missed. Suffice it to say that such
mementos serve as vital reminders of your ability to love and be loved;
they symbolize positive, if bittersweet, recollections. We are, rather,
referring to items that make you feel bad about yourself and your life
for any reason: a favorite necktie worn to a job from which you were

later fired would fall into this category, as would a framed photograph of yourself ten years ago, completely in shape and weighing thirty or forty pounds less than you do now.

After you have removed any negative mementos, place positive memorabilia around the rooms or areas in which you live and work. Ideal examples would include a piece of furniture you designed and built yourself, a plastic chip commemorating your third successful year as a member of Alcoholics Anonymous, or a rock you found deep in the bottom of your boot when you returned from successfully climbing Mount Everest. Such personal "trophies" can serve to inspire you to become a kind of positive role model for yourself in the future.

> **Mental Note**—A colleague of ours recommends choosing an animal with which you personally identify, and placing a representation of this animal somewhere in your everyday environment. You might for example, think of yourself as a powerful "bear," a graceful "swan," or a patriotic "eagle." While placing a stuffed animal or photograph representing your chosen creature somewhere in your home or office is not strictly a memory-related exercise, we still consider this approach worth mentioning because it can be psychologically beneficial. To carry this suggestion a step further, our colleague also recommends entering a state of alert relaxation and allowing an image of a personally meaningful animal to come to you while deeply relaxed.

> **Mental Note**—Read ahead through the rest of the instructions for Day 28 before carrying them out.

In part two of today's exercise, you'll turn your attention toward the future. Begin by finding a comfortable place to relax and enter a state of alert relaxation. Once you are deeply relaxed, imagine looking back on your present life from five years in the future. What sorts of mementos might surround your future self in homage to the life you are living now? Which objects will trigger positive recollections, and which ones, negative recollections? Overall, are you living the kind of everyday life which you will enjoy looking back on in the future?

After you have focused on these thoughts for at least ten minutes, continue to relax and clear your mind using the emptying technique you practiced during Week Three. Then imagine that you are reviewing your own life experiences ten years from now. With what sorts of mementos might you surround yourself to remind yourself of the kind of life you have lived since you were a child? Which objects might trigger positive recollections, and which ones might trigger negative recollections of your overall life experience? Maintain this focus for another ten minutes.

Finally, clear your mind once more and imagine looking back over your life from the perspective of twenty years in the future. Are there aspects of your "remembered" life that you would have lived differently if you could only "relive" the past? After maintaining this focus for another ten minutes, gradually bring yourself back to ordinary waking awareness.

As you return to full waking awareness, imagine that you have just returned to your own "past" from twenty years in the future. Consider the fact that you are currently creating the life experiences that will later reside in your memory twenty years from now. In a very real sense, therefore, you still have the power to create the best possible future memories of your own present existence. You may also have the power to avoid some or all of the "regrets" envisioned when you imagined yourself looking back over your life from five, ten, and twenty years in the future.

Complete today's exercise by choosing some psychologically fulfilling experience that you would like to remember in the future, but that you ordinarily might not allow yourself to take the time to enjoy. Spend as much of today as you can actually treating yourself to that experience. You may, for example, wish to spend the afternoon taking a carriage ride with a group of your friends through a city park, or having a gourmet picnic at the beach with one special person. You may like to take your first skydiving lesson, go scuba diving in the Pacific Ocean, or ice-skating in Rockefeller Center. Or you may simply like to spend part of today making arrangements for a vacation in some exotic country or shopping for some special clothes. Just be sure that you really follow through on any plans you make for yourself today, rather than simply going through the motions. And also be sure to bring home some suitable memento to remind you of this special experience in the future.

As you complete Day 28 of the Total-Recall Program, consider the fact that you are continuously sculpting your future memories during every moment of your life. It is always worthwhile to take some time to live the kind of life you will want to remember as you continue transforming the future into the past. On this note, we offer you our congratulations! You've just completed Week Four of the Total-Recall Program.

WEEK FOUR   TOTAL RECALL

DAY 22 THE AMAZING TECHNICOLOR DREAMCOAT			DAY 23 INNER OLFACTION
Consider the possible influence that objects and images within your sleep environment may have on your dreams. Make your dream environment as comfortable and nurturing as possible, removing any disturbing or intrusive images that might interfere with dream exploration. Introduce background stimuli into your sleep environment that will gently nudge you toward a gentle recollection of material you seek to remember. Place your dream diary,	special pen, and penlight in a prominent spot beside the bed. As you prepare for sleep, focus on the information you hope to recall and gently exclude all other thoughts from your mind. Calmly tell yourself that you will find the forgotten information in your dream and will remember it upon awakening. Write a phrase about the information you seek in your dream diary. As you fall asleep, continue focusing on the phrase you've written and picture any	relevant objects you may have placed around the room. Gently remind yourself to dream about the information you wish to recall and to remember any relevant dreams when you wake up. Practice dream-recollection techniques and record your dreams in your dream diary upon awakening.	Go to a department store that features large displays of perfumes and colognes. Take a mental inventory of the scents available for sampling. Notice whether any of the perfumes or colognes were used by some significant person from your past. Choose a scent that strikes you as particularly significant. If you cannot locate by name a familiar brand, sample some unfamiliar scents until one strikes you as familiar. Hold the sample close to *(continued)*

WEEK FOUR TOTAL RECALL (continued)

DAY 23 INNER OLFACTION	DAY 24 MEMORY TRACKS

DAY 23 — INNER OLFACTION

your nose and gently inhale the fragrance. Take care not to splash any of the liquid on your skin or clothes.

Take a few moments to appreciate the overall impact and underlying qualities of the scent you have chosen.

Close your eyes and immerse yourself in any images evoked by the scent as fully and emotionally as possible.

Open your eyes, reseal the sample, and practice the same exercise with a second scent, taking a 10- to 15-minute break between each sample.

Leave the store. Find a quiet place to sit and ask yourself how your reaction to a stranger wearing one of the scents you've sampled would be tempered by conscious or unconscious associations to the past.

As you go about the rest of the day, tune in to the scents associated with the people, places, and things around you. Ask yourself whether any remind you of the past.

DAY 24 — MEMORY TRACKS

Find a location where you can comfortably sit and observe the comings and goings of a wide variety of people.

Choose an appropriate vantage point and sit quietly for at least 30 minutes, calmly observing the passing parade.

Consider the ways in which total strangers trigger recollections of people who have played significant roles in your past.

Ask yourself if there are any personality qualities that you can acccurately predict based upon the unconscious cues

to which you are responding. Also consider the ways in which these cues might mislead you.

During the later part of your day, go to some other public place, and spend at least 30 minutes interacting with—or just observing— the people around you.

Compare these new faces to people from the past.

DAY 25 GORILLAS IN THE MIST	**DAY 26** INTUITIVE MEMORY

Visit the ape and monkey exhibits at your local zoo or rent or purchase a videotape featuring primate behavior in the wild.

Make sure you have a pad of paper and a pen or pencil.

Take at least one or two hours to carefully observe the behavior and interactions of these evolutionary antecedents. Try to make some judgments as to the basic personalities at play.

Ask yourself if the behavior of any of the individual primates reminds you of anyone you have ever known.

Sketch a picture of the primate that has evoked the strongest response. Alongside that first sketch, sketch the human individual who most reminds you of the monkey or ape.

Leave the primate exhibit or simply turn off your VCR.

As you go about the rest of your day, study new acquaintances as well as old friends and colleagues, much as you studied the primates. Look for facial and behavioral clues to their deeper drives and emotions.

Before you go to bed, take

your sketch pad and sketch the people you observed earlier in the day. Emphasize the facial expressions noted before.

Next to each drawing, sketch a monkey or an ape with that same prominent expression or characteristic.

Take the same pad and pen or pencil that you used yesterday to a comfortable location where you can concentrate without being interrupted.

On a blank piece of paper, write down a one-sentence description of some significant event in which you decided to act based on a seemingly "irrational" instinct.

Take 5 or 10 minutes to remember what was happening in your life before the situation in question. Briefly write down your recollections.

(continue)

WEEK FOUR TOTAL RECALL (continued)

DAY 26 INTUITIVE MEMORY	DAY 27 MEMORY BANKS	DAY 28 MEMORY SCULPTING	
Consider this memory exercise focusing on at least two more significant life events. Consider the ways in which your memories of these past experiences have provided you with any insights into your own intuitive or right-brain memory processes.	Begin preserving your memories by keeping a journal and collecting mementos from significant occasions. Make at least part of your residence a shrine to your memories, a place where you keep your old letters and personal journals, old pictures and mementos, videos and audiotapes. Start investing in your memory bank today.	Stop and consider the ephemeral nature of your journey through life. Take a mental inventory of the memorabilia with which you currently surround yourself in your home, office, or any other personally significant locale. Consider the ways in which many of the props that form the backdrop of your daily life spontaneously trigger memories of the past. Remove any negative mementos from your everyday environment. Place positive forms of mem-	orabilia around the rooms or areas in which you live and work. Find a comfortable place to relax and enter a state of alert relaxation. Once you are deeply relaxed, imagine looking back on your present life from five years in the future. Focus on these thoughts for at least ten minutes. Continue to relax and clear your mind using the emptying technique. Then imagine that you are reviewing your own life experiences 10 years from now. Maintain this focus for

another 10 minutes.

Clear your mind once more and imagine looking back over your life from the perspective of 20 years from now. After maintaining this focus for another ten minutes, gradually bring yourself back to ordinary waking awareness.

Imagine that you have just returned to your own "past" from 20 years in the future. Consider the fact that you are currently creating the life experiences that will later reside in your memory 20 years from now.

Choose some psychologically fulfilling experience that you would like to remember in the future, but that you ordinarily might not allow yourself to take the time to enjoy.

Spend as much of today as you can actually treating yourself to that experience.

Consider the fact that you are continuously sculpting your future memories during every day of your life.

DAYS 29 AND 30

MEMORY
IMPLANTS

What if you suddenly developed amnesia and no longer remembered any of the personal details of your past or present life? As you struggled to regain a sense of personal identity and create a meaningful life for yourself, which aspects of your personality do you think would remain immutable? Which aspects might be subject to dramatic change? If you had a traumatic childhood, for example, but had somehow eradicated that memory, could you come to believe that your childhood had actually been carefree and emotionally satisfying? If so, how would this alternative perspective influence your view of your actual present and possible future? If you had always been hopelessly unsuccessful with the opposite sex but, lacking any memory of this fact, accepted the notion that you were actually a sexual bon vivant with a varied and extensive history of colorful sexual encounters, how would this illusion influence your present self-image and behavior?

These questions may, at first, seem inconsequential to your own life. But when you consider how subjective your perspective on your life is anyway, they take on new meaning. Indeed, you may well have "amnesia" when it comes to recalling certain aspects of your past. Your view of reality may, in fact, be colored by your own unique perspective and window on the world. In fact, there are any number of people whose life histories are filled with parental abuse, incest, rejection, and unrelenting hard times. Yet while some of these people are driven past the boundaries of psychosis, others manage to survive emotionally intact and even to thrive. If there is a recognizable difference between those in the former group and those in the latter, it may be in their ability to subjectively—and positively—redefine their views of the past.

What is possible for these people is, with some effort, possible for the rest of us: On Days 29 and 30 you will attempt to generate positive memories that will enhance—as opposed to detract from—your present life.

Mental Note—Read ahead through the rest of the instructions for Days 29 and 30 before carrying them out. Again, we do not recommend this exercise as a form of psychotherapy. If you have any doubts about your ability to complete this exercise comfortably on your own, we recommend

that you seek the guidance and assistance of a sympathetic psycho-
therapist or that you simply skip this exercise altogether.

Begin the exercise for Days 29 and 30 by entering a private environment in which you can comfortably induce a state of alert relaxation.
Once you are deeply relaxed, allow a stream of memories to move
through your mind—almost as though you're watching a series of video
clips from someone else's life story. If you notice yourself getting stuck
on any particular memory, simply take a few moments to practice the
emptying exercise you learned in Week Three. Then turn your attention
back toward reviewing your memories from an emotional distance.

After you have carried out the first portion of this exercise for at
least fifteen minutes, you are ready to create a memory implant—a
single, fabricated event or an entire "imaginary past." For the next
fifteen minutes, imagine that one of the memories you reviewed never
actually occurred.

> ***Mental Note***—In general, it's best to choose a negative memory at this
> juncture. But you may choose any memory you wish. You may even
> envision away your entire childhood.

After you have visualized your real memories away, imagine a
replacement—ideally a more positive or fulfilling scenario than the one
you actually recalled having lived. As you deepen the memory replacement, notice the effect that this imaginary past has on your emotions
and your point of view. Envision what you believe may be possible for
you in the future, based upon this imaginary past.

As you begin returning to a state of ordinary waking awareness,
carry the new, fabricated memory—the memory implant—with you in
your head. As you go about the rest of the day, live and act as if this
new, altered memory had actually occurred. In fact, carry this memory
implant with you throughout Days 29 and 30.

Just before you go to bed on Day 30, let go of your imaginary past
and recall, once more, the actual, historical events of your life. As you
do so, ask yourself if there were aspects of your imaginary past that
corresponded with familiar aspects of who you are today. Consider the
positive future you envisioned for yourself after mentally recreating
your past. Then consider the possibility that your future can be just as
positive despite the unpleasant memories that may have influenced you
in the past.

As you move irrevocably toward the future, we wish you many
wonderful and fulfilling memories to come. We also extend our congratulations! You've just graduated from the Total-Recall Program.

APPENDIX A
A SPECIAL NOTE TO THE PHYSICALLY DISABLED

*F*or the sake of simplicity, the instructions for many of the exercises in the Total-Recall Program appear to assume certain basic physical capabilities. We sincerely hope, however, that the Total-Recall Program will attract a diverse readership, including many individuals who may have a wide variety of physical disabilities. In fact, there is absolutely no reason why the techniques presented in the Total-Recall Program cannot be practiced by everyone.

In much of our research at the Institute for Advanced Psychology, disabled individuals have made a significant contribution to our exploration and understanding of a wide range of extended human capabilities. We therefore request that our disabled readers bear with us, and that they feel free to adapt the various Total-Recall exercises to their personal capabilities and preferences.

We suggest, for example, that if you are blind, hearing imparied, usually in a wheelchair, or otherwise restricted in your ability to easily move around your environment, you simply adjust the exercises to your particular needs; we assure you that the program will work just as well. We also remind you that many of the Total-Recall exercises are easily adaptable to a wide variety of available sensory and psychological approaches. If necessary, it is completely acceptable to skip a particular exercise, simply replacing it with another more suited to your requirements on a particular day. It is also always acceptable to proceed at a pace that feels most comfortable for you and works best in your individual situation.

We thank you for your interest and participation in the Total-Recall Program. We hope it will add a new dimension of enriching inner exploration and experience to your life.

—Keith Harary and Pamela Weintraub

APPENDIX B
FURTHER READING

Csikszentmihalyi, Mihaly, *Flow: The Psychology of Optimal Experience*. New York: HarperPerrenial, 1991.

Harary, Keith, Ph.D., and Pamela Weintraub, *Higher Consciousness in 30 Days: The Mystical Experience Programme*. London: The Aquarian Press, 1991.

Harary, Keith, Ph.D., and Pamela Weintraub, *Lucid Dreams in 30 Days: The Creative Sleep Programme*. London: The Aquarian Press, 1990.

Rico, Gabriele, *Writing the Natural Way*. Los Angeles: Tarcher, 1983.

Squire, Larry R, B. Hers and Nelson, *The Neuropsychology of Memory*. New York: Guilford Press, 1984.

ACKNOWLEDGMENTS

We wish to express our sincere gratitude to our spouses: Darlene Moore, who makes other women fade from memory, and Mark Teich, who remembers with the best of them.

We would also like to thank our colleagues and friends who have helped us to gain a deeper understanding of the many dimensions of memory, especially those whose expertise we have drawn upon in developing the Total-Recall Program. Our very special appreciation to our friend and colleague George Kokoris, M.D., Ph.D., for his invaluable insights and suggestions; Barbara Rubin, Ph.D., for her special advice and wisdom; and to Rene Van de Carr, M.D., of Prenatal University; Thomas Verney, M.D.; and Gabriele Rico, Ph.D. We would like to acknowledge *Omni* magazine, where variations of some of the Total-Recall exercises first appeared.

Special thanks also goes to our talented and supportive editor, Robert Weil, who came up with the 30-day concept, and Richard Romano of St. Martin's Press, for his great sense of humor and additional support. We would also like to express our sincere appreciation to our literary agents, Roslyn Targ and Wendy Lipkind.

We also extend our appreciation to the board of directors and board of scientific advisers of the Institute for Advanced Psychology for their role in furthering advanced psychological research.

ABOUT THE AUTHORS

Keith Harary, Ph.D., is internationally known for his pioneering contributions to scientific research on altered states of consciousness and extended human abilities. Dr. Harary, who holds a Ph.D. in psychology with emphasis in both clinical counseling and experimental psychology, has authored and co-authored more than sixty popular and professional articles on topics relating to advanced psychological research and other areas. His work has been discussed in dozens of scientific and popular publications and more than three dozen books. He is also coauthor, with Pamela Weintraub, of *Have an Out-of-Body Experience in 30 Days: The Free Flight Programme; Lucid Dreams in 30 Days: The Creative Sleep Programme; Higher Consciousness in 30 Days: The Mystical Experience Programme; Inner Sex in 30 Days: The Erotic Fulfilment Programme;* and *Right-Brain Learning in 30 Days: The Whole Mind Programme*. He is also coauthor of the best-selling book *The Mind Race*. He is president and research director of the Institute for Advanced Psychology in San Francisco.

Pamela Weintraub is editor-at-large of *Omni* magazine, where she has worked on staff for the past ten years. She is also the author or coauthor of nine previous books, including *Nurturing the Unborn Child, You Can Save the Animals*, and *25 Things You Can Do to Beat the Recession of the 1990s*. She is coauthor, with Keith Harary, of the books in the *30 Days* series (see above). Her articles have appeared in many national magazines from *Omni* to *Health* to *Discover*.

We would like to hear about your experience with the Total-Recall Programme. Please contact us at:

The Institute for Advanced Psychology
Box 875
2269 Chestnut Street
San Francisco, CA
94123
USA

By the same authors . . .

RIGHT-BRAIN LEARNING IN 30 DAYS

Right-brain learning rallies the powers of your intuitive and nonverbal right brain to help you better absorb all kinds of new information in your personal and professional life. Opening up right-brain channels of learning should make you much more adept at absorbing new concepts and mastering complex skills that simply bogged you down before.

- Do you tend to approach new challenges in a logical, sequential, step-by-step way, sometimes missing the big picture while focusing on the small details?

- Do you tend to tense up when learning a new subject, finding it difficult to focus and to become completely immersed in the topic at hand due to outside distractions?

- Do you tend to get stumped when studying such technical subjects as accounting or organic chemistry, finding it difficult to make connections between abstract symbols and the concepts they represent?

Even if you're an excellent student and have enjoyed great personal and professional success, you can still benefit from Harary and Weintraub's exercises as a means of enhancing the prowess of your right brain and your overall ability to learn.

HAVE AN OUT-OF-BODY EXPERIENCE IN 30 DAYS	1 85538 002 1	☐	£4.99
HIGHER CONSCIOUSNESS IN 30 DAYS	1 85538 122 2	☐	£4.99
INNER SEX IN 30 DAYS	1 85538 121 4	☐	£4.99
LUCID DREAMS IN 30 DAYS	1 85538 003 X	☐	£4.99
RIGHT-BRAIN LEARNING IN 30 DAYS	1 85538 241 5	☐	£4.99

All these books are available at your local bookseller or can be ordered direct from the publishers.

To order direct just tick the titles you want and fill in the form below:

Name: _____

Address: _____

_____

_____ Post Code: _____

Send to: Thorsons Mail Order, Dept 3A, HarperCollinsPublishers, Westerhill Road, Bishopbriggs, Glasgow G64 2QT.

Please enclose a cheque or postal order or debit my Visa/Access account —

Credit card no: _____

Expiry date: _____

Signature: _____

— to the value of the cover price plus:

UK & BFPO: Add £1.00 for the first book and 25p for each additional book ordered.

Overseas orders including Eire: Please add £2.95 service charge. Books will be sent by surface mail but quotes for airmail despatches will be given on request.

24 HOUR TELEPHONE ORDERING SERVICE FOR ACCESS OR VISA CARDHOLDERS — TEL **041 772 2281**